F. S. Adams.

A LIFE'S MOTTO.

ILLUSTRATED BY

Biographical Examples.

Drawn by J. D. WATSON.

A LIFE'S MOTTO.

LIFE'S MOTTO.

ILLUSTRATED BY

Biographical Examples.

"WHATSOEVER THY HAND FINDETH TO DO, DO IT WITH THY MIGHT; for there is no work, nor device, nor knowledge, nor wisdom, in the grave, whither THOU goest."

BY THE

REV. THOMAS PELHAM DALE, M.A.

RECTOR OF ST. VEDAST WITH ST. MICHAEL,
AND LATE FELLOW OF SIDNEY COLLEGE, CAMBRIDGE.

WITH A FRONTISPIECE BY J. D. WATSON.

NEW YORK:
VIRTUE AND YORSTON, PUBLISHERS.

CONTENTS.

WESLEY, THE METHODIST.

Faith arousing the slumbering Church.

JOHN NEWTON, THE CONVERTED SLAVE-DRIVER.

Faith victorious over blaspheming Atheism.

EDWARD IRVING, THE ENTHUSIAST.

Faith in Credulity.

HENRY MARTYN AND CHARLES FREDERICK MACKENZIE, THE MARTYR MISSIONARIES.

Faith loving not Life unto Death.

INTRODUCTION.

"Nor is it only at the close of the pilgrimage that the hope full of immortality is a pearl of great price. Without it, life is so transient, that every invention is a melancholy plaything, and the vastest acquirements are a laborious futility. But the student who toils for immortality need never want a motive in his work; and, however sad some of his discoveries may be, the sage who knows the Saviour will always have in his knowledge an overplus of joy."—JAMES HAMILTON: *The Royal Preacher.*

"Go thy way, then; eat with pleasure thy bread, and drink thy wine with joyful heart, if at this present God prospers thy work. In every season (if thou canst), put on the garment of rejoicing, and do not restrain the expression of thy gladness. Enjoy to the utmost thy life, in companionship with her whom thou lovest—all the days of thy transitory life which may be granted thee in this hot, work-day world; for this is all thou canst have as thy portion in life, and in all that toil thyself art toiling at in this hot, work-day world. All that thy power enables thee to do, do it with all thy strength; for there is neither work, nor device, nor knowledge, nor wisdom, in Hades; and that is whither THOU art going."—*Ecc.* ix. 7-10, *paraphrased.*

A LIFE'S MOTTO.

INTRODUCTION.

HE life's motto of our title-page has been diversely understood. As ordinarily quoted, and apart from its context, it has been regarded as a simple exhortation to diligence: "Do what you have to do in earnest," and be successful; and, so understood, it is, in its way, a very good motto. But it is more than doubtful if this is what the writer had in view. When we come to examine the context, we perceive that he is rather undervaluing diligence than otherwise. He takes immediate occasion to remind his auditors that "the race is not always to the swift, nor the battle to the strong, nor the bread to the wise, nor wealth to the prudent;" while, again, the reason he gives for being so diligent in what one's hand finds

to do, is about the last one would have expected, if attainment of success had been the object in view. To tell a man to work hard because in this manner much may be accomplished, is one thing; but to tell him to work hard because there is so little time in which to work, is something very different. Yet this is what we have here; diligence is recommended, not because it is needed to command success, but because there is so very little time to do any thing at all.

Thus it happens that some have been inclined to read the passage in the sense of the Epicurean motto: "A short life and a merry one." Others would put the passage in inverted commas, and look upon it as a quotation—the words of a sceptic, cited for refutation. Others, again, seeing plainly that the whole sermon is an intensely earnest exhortation to a godly life, have characterised such passages as this as "the fitful meditations of one who knows better."

The true solution of this difficulty is to be found in the character of the book itself, which is a sermon full of paradoxes. These paradoxes allure into attention by their strange and enigmatical utterances, and then strike into the conscience when the listener is thus taken off his guard. The writer is a consummate master of spiritual sarcasm—one who wields, with amazing dexterity, the two-edged sword of the Spirit, and cuts you sharp with its back edge. You think the blow has passed you, or even been taken at random, and, lo! it whirls round, and cuts you to the quick. And our motto will, when we come to examine it, be found to be one of these back-handed blows. A superficial reading might lead you to suppose that it sets forth diligence in this life because this life is all; really, it bids you look altogether beyond it.

Let us suppose, then, that a hearer of the sermon, inclined to scepticism, but not quite comfortable in his scepticism,—as few are,—took this passage home with him, as a crumb of comfort in favour of his views; he might surely meditate upon it thus: The advice to live happily is, as human nature goes, with one's very few opportunities of following it, somewhat sarcastic. To tell one to enjoy at all times what only a few can enjoy seldom,—and many not at all,—is like the advice which physicians have been known to give, when some over-worked son of toil—poisoned by the noisomeness of his own trade, and who must either work or starve—comes to them for medicine. They tell him medicine will do no good, that he must have perfect rest, and the delights of a country retreat. There is a mocking undertone of "If you can," in such advice. Then, again, the preacher harps continually on the transitoriness of life, even in the midst of his vivid description of its pleasures. In this banquet, the skeleton is so very prominent,—the passage is a kind of Dance of Death. By dexterous word-painting, it leads us on, through the description of the feast, in order to land us in the darkness of the grave. True, the preacher enjoins haste and diligence; but what is it to end in? Not in success—he says nothing about that; he really intimates that the time is so short, and the end so near, that at the best there will hardly be time for enjoyment at all. Yes, we may imagine our sceptic saying to himself, it's just what you might expect from a preacher. He feigns to join in the mirth, that he may improve the occasion. He speaks about the joys of life, only to introduce allusions to its shortness; and tells you to enjoy yourself to the utmost, only to make you feel the more keenly the black, dark disappointment such a life is altogether,—to remind you that, under the sun of this hot world of toil, there is no work of which you can have any lasting profit,—no device which will give you any permanent advantage,—no knowledge by which you may prolong life,—no wisdom by which you may postpone your entrance into that world of forgetfulness whither you are hastening.

The truth, then, really is, that these words teach just the very reverse of what a careless and superficial reading would draw from them. They are enigmatical, no doubt, but not so enigmatical but that they may be readily understood. After all, they are only the Apostle's caution, to "use this world as not abusing it, for the fashion of this world passeth away," —written in character a little ornamented and flourished withal, but only just so difficult of decipherment as to enhance the impression the aphorism is intended to produce. It is, in cipher-form, the great maxim of the divine life: The time is short,—live for the higher existence. It is a prelude intended to work up to that which is to be the conclusion of the whole matter: "Fear God, and keep His commandments; for this is the whole duty of man."

Keeping this in view, it will be a matter of no surprise that the biographical illustrations which follow are not the annals of men who, simply diligent, were successful; nor do we think there is much need of such biographies, least of all in an age like ours, where success often succeeds far better than principle. What will be found here are examples of men who were indeed eminently successful, but not in the worldly sense of that word,—men who did what they did with all their might, because they knew that the grave, and its forgetfulness, were only the limits of the worldly life under the sun, and not at all the limits of the spiritual existence. It is true that, in a sense, all Christian men are such as these; but the success of those men whose lives are here set forth, arose not so much from the earnestness of their labours, as from the depth of their convictions. The key-note is struck in the first biography, that of Augustine. In his *Confessions*, we have a self-analysis, by one of the greatest masters of human thought, of the process and progress of the great change, as it occurred in his own heart, and within the range of his own experience. Few men, before their conversion, have loved the world more,—few men, after it, have loved the world less, and done more for it. All the other biographies tell a similar tale. They are the histories of men who had all gone through the same experiences, and had the same kind of success. In a word, they were first converted themselves, and then began to convert others; except, indeed, Kirke White, who died before his time, destroyed by his own over-haste in the path of duty, and who is added to illustrate the truth, that "the race is not always to the swift, nor the battle to the strong." But in them all we can trace the operation of the Spirit of God; and, in consequence, there is a certain striking sameness in these biographies. The men all think alike, speak alike, and, in the same circumstances, act alike. Unity of faith and hope begets unity of thought and life. They are all brethren; and there is a marvellous family likeness amongst these sons of God.

The principal modern biographies have all been drawn from one school of religious thought: not that by doing this the author would be supposed to intimate that in this school alone are to be found high illustrations of the true principles of religious life, but because thus, without departing from the main object he had in view, he could throw light upon an important period in the history of our Church. It is much to be wished that some calm, impartial, and well-read writer would now undertake a history of the Evangelical revival of the last century. The force of that revival is no doubt spent, and the Church is at present stirred with new modes of thought; the great river of truth, in its course from beneath the temple, has in our time made a visible bend: but this is the period when a review may be taken of the progress already made, before the new vista comes into sight. To contribute towards a page of this history seemed to be just now important. No one can doubt that these men, whose biographies are here set forth, were the spiritual fathers of the present generation of religious thinkers. Whether they know it or not, there is something of the Wesleyan and Simeonite about them all. Wesley woke up the Church of England to a sense of its duties and its position. The leading preachers of the last generation were in methods and topics, if not by direct instruction, "Sims."* The great doctrines which sounded novel in their days, and which they spent their lives in enforcing, were: Christ's death upon the cross, the only satisfaction for man's sin; and the universal necessity for conversion to be evidenced by holiness of life. But these doctrines are not novel now; they sound out from almost every pulpit in the land. If, then, the force of this revival be spent, it is because the work these men of God had to do is so far done; not because these doctrines are effete, or have lost their power,—that is impossible; they are founded on the everlasting hills, and will endure as long. If other doctrines now need to be enforced, it can only be by way of addition,

* The term is explained at page 200.

and not of substitution, by bringing into prominence side by side with these, and without obscuring them, what in that age were either less necessary, or were overlooked. When, also, it is seen how much alike Augustine and Wesley and Simeon are in principles and practice, it will be perceived that these two last are not so deficient in "Catholic principles" as some nowadays seem to imagine.

That these men of God sometimes erred, is not denied. That they preached the whole counsel of God, without undue exaltation of one side or the other; that all topics were handled with equal skill, or enforced with equal fervour; or that their theological system was so perfect as to leave nothing to be desired, —can only be true of those who wrote by direct inspiration of the Spirit of God, and therefore not of these. No, they were men, uninspired men, and with all the faults of men; and in this circumstance is to be discovered one of the most consolatory of lessons: it shows the power of grace to perfect and sanctify characters which nevertheless remained to the very end the same. The writer of such a biography has no occasion to make his heroes too excellent or faultless; indeed, all biographies which conceal the man's faults are as fictitious as novels, without the advantage of a plot or catastrophe; but religious biographies so written give an impression altogether false. The power of grace is shown, not by the destruction of the individuality of its subject, but by his improvement and progressive sanctification. The religion of Augustine and Monica—beautiful and genuine as it is—is, nevertheless, not without a taint of superstition; yet, as their Christian characters mature, they rise more and more conspicuously above the weaknesses of their age. Beneath the cowl of Bernard, where some would only expect to find a dry, self-torturing asceticism, is as genuine a Christianity as the world ever witnessed. Wesley was self-opinionated and fond of power, and Simeon self-conscious and vain; but they both of them loved the Gospel which they preached. They were none the better for these failings; they introduced, in consequence, a corrupt leaven into their work, which produced so far evil results. But this must be the history of every religious movement. This leaven must be hid in the three measures of meal, or they will never become tasty loaves, fit for the festive table; but the great Head of the Church knows when the corruption has proceeded far enough, and arrests it at the proper moment, so bringing good out of evil. In every age, more or less of human error has been mixed with the divine work,—and no doubt the Evangelical revival was no exception; but it had preëminently hold of those great central truths of which we have spoken, and which constituted the secret of its power—a power which is retained undiminished to this moment, as mighty in the nineteenth century as in the first; for not more certain is it that the darkness of night disappears before the rising of the sun, than that the darkness of infidelity or indifferentism will be dispersed, and an awakening to new religious life occur, wherever and however is faithfully preached repentance towards God, and faith in our Lord Jesus Christ.

AUGUSTINE, BISHOP OF HIPPO.

Faith's great Victory over Heathenism.

"The great cement which holds these several discourses together is one main design which they jointly drive at, and which, I think, is confessedly generous and important—the knowledge of true happiness, so far as reason can cut her way through those darknesses and difficulties one is incumbered with in this life."—Henry More.

LIFE OF AUGUSTINE, BISHOP OF HIPPO.

URELIUS AUGUSTINUS—or, as he is usually called, Augustine—was born at Tagaste, in Numidia, November 13th, A.D. 353. His father, Patricius Augustinus, was a pagan, a man of strong passions and violent temper. His mother, Monica, was a Christian maiden, only just of marriageable age when she was united to Patricius.

The married life of Monica, though happy in the main, was, as might be expected, not without its trials. Patricius, in the earlier period of their married life, proved but an indifferent husband. Much of his time was spent with his heathen companions, from whose society he would often return in a temper, only to find fault with and storm at his gentle wife. He was unfaithful, and sometimes cruel; on occasion, it appears, he would even strike her. Her true, earnest, and persevering piety enabled her to find a remedy for all this. She learned, when reviled, not to answer again; but if her husband stormed, she would remain silent, until, in calmer moments, he could listen to reason, when she would with loving gentleness win him by her pleadings. She was also careful never to complain; but where other matrons, with less cause than she had, would angrily proclaim their wrongs, she kept faithfully the secret of her husband's unkindnesses. She would win him over by patient submissiveness and unfailing love. This, joined with earnest prayer for his conversion, she maintained during the whole of their married life; and she succeeded. Patricius at length became a convert to that Christianity which shone out in such bright and loving characters in his wife's life. The year before his death, he enrolled himself among the catechumens, and made public profession of the Christian faith by baptism.

Another domestic trial was found in the peevish and irritable temper of the mother of Patricius, who was an inmate of Monica's household, and disturbed the peace of the family by listening to, and disseminating, idle and scandalous tales of her daughter-in-law. Monica, on her side, met this by such persevering endurance and meekness, that she succeeded in converting a suspicious enemy into a dear and attached friend,—so that they henceforth lived together in remarkable sweetness and mutual kindness.

Monica is, in her quiet, womanly way, a brilliant

example of unvarying and persevering faith—an instance both of a devoted woman and a woman of devotion. For thirty years, day and night, often with strong supplication and tears, strong in faith, she held on, praying for the conversion of her son. Yet all this time she never despaired, never complained or murmured against God, assured that these prayers would one day be answered. Nor was she disappointed. In due time, mother-in-law, husband, children were granted to her, until she had lived just long enough to see them all earnest and devoted Christians.

A picturesque incident in the life of Monica gives us a curious insight into the domestic relations of a Christian family of those times. Monica, as we have already noticed, was brought up by Christian parents. It was not, however, so much by her mother's teaching, as through that of an aged servant, that she learned her lessons of piety and self-control. The old woman had, when quite a girl, carried Monica's father "as big girls use to do who carry the little ones on their backs," says Augustine. This long-standing attachment, begun in childhood, together with her now great age and godly conversation, caused her to be greatly honoured by her master and mistress, so that to her was committed the care of the children. To this she gave diligent heed, restraining them earnestly with a holy severity when that was necessary, and teaching them always with grave sobriety. Perhaps, indeed, according to our modern notions, she may have been a little over-strict; for, except at those times when they were furnished with the very temperate allowance of wine permitted at their parents' table, she would not allow them, though very thirsty, to drink even water, guarding against an evil habit, and adding this wholesome advice: "You drink water now," said she, "because you cannot get wine. When you are married, and come to have cellars and cupboards of your own, you will despise water; but the habit of drinking will remain." Instructing them in this manner, and using her authority, she restrained the greediness of childhood, and so formed in these girls such excellent habits of moderation, that they would of their own accord take no more than they ought.

Nevertheless, Monica was in danger of falling into the evil habit of drinking; for when she was sent, as often happened, to the cellar to draw wine, being regarded by her parents as a sober maiden, she would sometimes treat herself to a little sip before she poured the wine into the flagon: at first a very little sip,—for she was too honest to take much, and acted rather through childish thoughtlessness than from any desire to drink. The evil habit, as may be anticipated, grew with indulgence. By degrees learning to take a little more, she at length fell into the habit of greedily swallowing a cup almost brimful of wine. A maid-servant, with whom she used to go to the cellar, happening to have a quarrel with her, taunted her, when they were alone, with this fault, calling her little mistress, in a very insulting way, a tippler. This taunt stung her to the quick. She acknowledged her fault, and never repeated it.

Such, then, was the character of the parents by whom Augustine was brought up. As an infant, he seems to have been passionate, squalling lustily if he could not have his own way; as a boy, quick and clever, but often in trouble on account of his idleness and love of play. This brought on the punishment of the rod; of this punishment he was in great terror, and would sometimes pray that he might be delivered from it. Speaking of this part of his life, he somewhat naively observes, that the teachers are often quite as much to blame as the pupils; for the same things which in children are sins against tutors and masters, about nuts and balls and sparrows, are in maturer years transformed into sins against magistrates and kings, about gold, estates, and slaves. According, then, to his own showing, we may say that he was a rather naughty boy than otherwise; yet not without some sense of the religion which he had been taught, and some boyish prayers and strivings after better things.

As he grew older, he certainly did not grow better. At the age of sixteen he fell into dissolute habits, which he describes thus: "I foamed out, a miserable creature, in the tide of my own passions, having forsaken Thee, O God, and overpassed all the bounds which Thou hast set. Yet I did not escape Thy scourges: for who of mortals can? Yet Thou wert ever present, mercifully wrathful, with very bitter checks dashing those unlawful pleasures of mine, so that I might rather seek those that were without alloy. But where to find such pleasures I could not discover, save in Thee, O Lord; in Thee, who makest our grief serve for our instruction; who woundest in order to heal, and killest us lest we should die to Thee." Never, then, was he without a sense of remorse. And there was this present advantage in his mother's early teaching,—it had awakened his conscience. If he sinned, he never could sin comfortably.

A fruitful cause of his fall, as he confesses, was idleness. At this time his studies were intermitted. He had returned from Madura, whither he had gone to learn grammar and rhetoric, and was waiting until the means could be furnished for a residence at Carthage, where he might have the greater advantages which a capital city could provide in the way of education. His father, being but a poor freeman of Tagaste, could only with difficulty provide the requisite money, "by his resolution rather than his means." He seems, however, to have, in this respect, thoroughly done his duty by his boy. Being a heathen, he thought but little of his son's irregularities; for he could easily look over any thing of this kind, if only he might at length see him rising to eminence as a first-rate speaker. He spoke of them lightly, almost approvingly, to Monica, as displaying a free and energetic spirit. She was now, however, a deep Christian—"the foundation of God's holy temple already begun in her heart;" and Augustine's sins filled her with anxiety and foreboding. She remonstrated tenderly and earnestly with him on the wrong he was doing; but at that time, as he confesses, to no purpose: he despised such remonstrances as womanish. Surrounded by wicked companions, he would even appear worse than he really was,—thus glorying in his shame. He mentions with especial regret, as one of the sins of his youth, a theft of which he was guilty at this period of his life. Near the house was a garden, in which was a pear-tree, the fruit of which was of a comparatively worthless kind. Augustine and some of his companions made a raid upon this tree in the night; but as they did not really care for the fruit, they threw it to the pigs. Many would have considered this circumstance in the light of a palliation, and looked upon the matter as a mere boyish freak. Not so Augustine: he seems to have been deeply impressed with remorse for this sin, as especially heinous by reason of its gratuitous character. "Behold, O God, my heart, which Thou pitiest when in the lowest depth. Let that heart say to Thee, Behold my heart. What did it seek there, that I should be gratuitously evil, having no motive for evil except the evil itself? It was foul, and yet I loved it, loved to perish, loved not that on account of which I committed the fault, but the fault itself. Foul soul, falling from Thy heaven into utter destruction, not seeking something by means of disgrace, but the disgrace itself!" Must we not say, when we calmly consider the real bearing of such sins, that Augustine is right in this very severe judgment of them?

At the age of seventeen he went to Carthage, where he formed a secret and illicit connection. He confesses that these sweet, stolen waters were dashed with gall and wormwood, and gave him no real pleasure. "I was scourged," he says, "with the burning iron rods of jealousy, and suspicion, and fears, and angers, and quarrels." About this time his father died. His mother, it appears, was left with sufficient means to continue his allowance at Carthage, and so enable him to go on with his studies. He determined to become a rhetorician, at that time considered, as we do the bar at the present day, an honourable and lucrative profession. He was a diligent and industrious student, at his nineteenth year attaining the honour of being the first in the rhetoric-school.

At this period he met with a work of Cicero's, now unfortunately lost, entitled *Hortensius*. By this book, though that of a heathen, a more serious turn was given to his thoughts than heretofore, so that from the perusal of this work he traces the beginning of those deeper convictions which at length resulted in his conversion. He now resolved to turn his mind to the study of Holy Scripture; but the style of Scripture, so utterly different from the artificial and flowing periods of Cicero, displeased him by its very simplicity. He was not yet in a frame of mind to relish a study into which one must enter as a little child, if any profit is to be received; but "I," says he, "disdained to be a little one; and, swollen with pride, took myself to be a great one."

Yet one brought up as Augustine was, and with a mind so powerful as his, must have some system in which to rest. He craved certainty in the midst of his doubts; and, to this end, he adopted that philosophy which in his day promised to make plain that which revelation hath left mysterious. He joined himself, accordingly, to the sect of the Manicheans. At that time, Manicheanism was an enemy to orthodox truth as powerful and dangerous as any the Church has ever contended against; though now so utterly dead and effete, that it is difficult to give the modern English reader even a notion of its peculiar tenets. To us it appears as a farrago of crude speculations on the divine nature and the origin of evil, joined with an absurd species of asceticism, which relapsed, with more than the ordinary rapidity of such asceticism, into utter licentiousness. It made, however, as these so-called philosophic systems are wont to do, loud promises of certainty to those who would adopt its teachings, professing to clear up that which previous philosophies had left doubtful, or divine revelation had passed over in silence. Then, again, it contained certain Pantheistic and Necessitarian doctrines, which, as they virtually implied a denial of human responsibility, so also implied a palliation of human sin; and such tenets are necessarily pleasing to those who, like Augustine at this time, are living a life morally below that standard which conscience prescribes to them.

To his mother, Monica, this relapse into absolute heresy was an awful grief: she looked upon it as a kind of spiritual death; she wept for him more than mothers weep the bodily deaths of their children. But her old resource of earnest prayer did not fail her. She wept and prayed so earnestly, that the ground on which she stood was wet with tears. Dearly as she loved him, she doubted whether she ought, even in his case, though her own son, to admit him to her house, or bid him God-speed, or, much as she delighted in his society, to eat bread with him at the same table. She was much comforted in her sorrow, however, by a dream. She saw herself standing upon a wooden measuring-rule, overwhelmed with grief and anxiety on account of her son, when a shining youth approached her, cheerful and smiling. He came up to her, and asked, as angels do who come to comfort, why she wept. She answered, that she was bewailing her son's loss. He bade her rest contented; and told her to look and see that, where she was, there was her son also. She looked, and saw Augustine standing at her side. Her simple faith regarded this dream as a divine intimation that all would yet be well; and she held fast hold of her persuasion, even when Augustine cavilled, and observed that the dream might just as well imply that she, on her part, should come over to his opinions.

She also entreated a good and learned bishop of her acquaintance to reason and expostulate with Augustine; but, although he was ready to argue with those whom he considered of a teachable disposition, he declined to do this in the case of her son; for he said that he was yet unteachable, being puffed up with the novelty of his heresy, and had perplexed divers unskilful persons with captious questions. "But let him alone," said he, "and only pray to the Lord for him, and he will some day find out for himself how great his error is, and what a wicked system he has adopted." He told her, also, that when he was young he had himself been consigned to the teaching of the Manicheans by his mother, who was a pervert to their doctrines, and that he had read and copied out most of their books; but, without any arguments, he had seen the falsehood of their system, and had left it. Monica was not satisfied with this, and still continued her importunity; when the old bishop got a little out of patience, and said: "Go thy way, and the Lord be with thee. It is not possible that the son of so many prayers can perish." She took this answer as a message sent from heaven.

Augustine continued a Manichean up to his eight-and-twentieth year; following, with some success, his profession of a rhetorician. About this time, an event occurred which impressed him much. This was the death of a very dear friend, who had been both his schoolmate and playmate, and the companion of his studies, and in part a convert, through his influence, to Manichean opinions. This young man fell sick of a fever; and, as he lay quite insensible, was baptised by his friends, who despaired of his recovery. Augustine imagined, naturally enough, that, should reason be restored, he would be more influenced by his arguments than by an act of which he was himself unconscious. The event proved quite otherwise; for, on his recovery from the fever, as soon as he was able to be spoken to, Augustine essayed to jest with him on the subject of his baptism. But his sick friend shrunk from Augustine as from an enemy; and, with a boldness and freedom as unexpected as it was unusual, bade him, if he would continue to be his friend, forbear such topics for the future. A few days after, his friend had a relapse, and died. Augustine's sorrow was deep and excessive —he had no hope. He then realised that a Saviour who was a phantom* was no Saviour for hours of sorrow, and that a philosophical system would as

* A doctrine of the Manicheans was, that the Lord who died on the cross was not really a man, but only the image or phantom of one.

little comfort mourners as save sinners. This shock apparently weakened his confidence in Manicheanism, though as yet it did not bring him to the truth.

Another circumstance occurred about a year after this, which also shook his confidence in the tenets he then held. Faustus, a bishop of the Manicheans, and greatly celebrated among his own sect, came to Carthage. Augustine was most anxious for an interview, expecting to obtain, from one of so great reputation, a solution of certain difficulties which he had encountered, and which appear to have arisen with regard to certain arithmetical or astronomical calculations which Augustine considered erroneous. The desired interview revealed to him that Faustus, although eloquent and pleasing in manner, was wholly deficient in real learning, and altogether a man of inferior capacity. He candidly told Augustine that he could not solve his difficulties, and confessed his entire ignorance of mathematics. Augustine, who had joined the sect in hopes of certainty, was proportionately disappointed at such a result.

About this time, Augustine determined to remove to Rome. The metropolis was a wider field, and would give more scope to his ambition than a provincial capital such as Carthage. His principal reason, however, was, that he hoped at Rome to avoid a set of noisy pupils, who at Carthage were accustomed to disturb the classes. His mother, no doubt fearing fresh temptation, was averse to his departure, and endeavoured to persuade him not to go, or, if otherwise, to allow her to accompany him. Augustine determined to go alone; and when Monica, suspecting his intention, insisted on going down to the shore with him, he persuaded her to enter a chapel near to the place of departure, and, while she was praying there, went on board secretly at night, and set sail. His mother was frantic with grief when she found herself alone and deserted. He thus affectingly describes this scene: "The wind blew, and filled our sails, and withdrew the shore from our sight; but there was she on the morrow frantic with sorrow, and with complainings and with groans filled Thy ears, O Lord, who despisest these groans; whilst Thou, by means of my lusts, wast hurrying me away, in order that Thou mightest take away these lusts. Meanwhile, Thou chastenest with the just punishment of her griefs what was carnal in her affection for me: for she loved to have me with her, as mothers are wont to do, and much more than most mothers; and she knew not how great joys Thou wert about to work out for her by my absence. She knew not, and therefore did she weep. And yet, after accusing my treachery and hard-heartedness, she betook herself to intercede with Thee for me,—went to her wonted place, and I to Rome."

At Rome he was seized with fever, which brought him to the very jaws of death. Had he departed, it would have been, as he intimates, an awful parting for ever; but he was spared to his mother's prayers. He recovered; and, though he still continued a Manichean, and did not break off with his evil practices, he was now approaching that great change which was to exert so deep an influence on himself and others. He became more and more dissatisfied with the tenets he had embraced, though as yet he made no open abjuration of them.

About this time, application was made to the Prefect of Rome to send to Milan, at the public expense, a reader in rhetoric. Augustine applied for the vacant chair, and, through the interest of some Manichean friends, obtained the appointment.

Here he met the celebrated Ambrose, Bishop of Milan, who received him with great kindness. Augustine had heard the eloquence of Ambrose highly spoken of, and attended his sermons, in order that he might judge for himself as to his merits as a speaker, but without at that time any intention of joining the Church. He was delighted with discourses which, while less winning and harmonious than those of Faustus, were far deeper and more earnest. By degrees this eloquence won upon him, until he became more and more impressed with the truth of what was spoken. At length he renounced his Manichean principles, and became a catechumen in the Catholic Church. His mother had now joined him, strong in her faith, following her son over land and sea, and in all her perils—for she narrowly escaped shipwreck—firmly trusting in her God. Augustine met her with the tidings that he was now no longer a Manichean, though not as yet a Catholic Christian. She expressed no surprise at the intelligence, but calmly replied: "I believe in Christ that, before I depart, I shall see thee a faithful Catholic." Nevertheless, she did not neglect to pray very earnestly for a speedy completion of the good work begun in him. A warm friendship speedily sprung up betwixt herself and Ambrose,—she naturally regarding him as the means through which was accomplished her son's conversion; he, on his side, attracted by her deep and unfeigned piety. He would, indeed, frequently burst forth into her praises to Augustine, congratulating him that he had such a mother.

Nevertheless, neither Ambrose nor Augustine knew much as yet of the other's inner life. The cares of an important diocese left Ambrose but little leisure; and on that little Augustine was diffident of intruding. Had he obtained, however, the private interview he desired, it is not likely that he would have been much benefited; for, as he confesses at this time, he was more anxious for disputation than conviction; beside which, he was still enslaved by passion. He panted after distinction, riches, marriage, but found nothing but disappointment. He confesses even to have envied the jollity of a half-drunken beggar, who for a while could steep the cares of his poverty in forgetfulness,—so uneasy and unhappy was he under the stings of a justly accusing conscience.

Monica especially desired to have him married, hoping thus to wean him from his irregular life. He was in consequence betrothed, chiefly through his mother's exertions, to a young maiden; but, as she was under age, it was judged expedient that two years should elapse before the marriage. In prospect of this, Augustine dismissed his concubine, who left him entirely, and afterwards led a strictly virtuous life. By her he had a son, Adeodatus, a lad of great promise, who remained with his father. Yet so great a slave was Augustine to passion, that soon after he took another concubine; but, as his *Confessions* reveal, not without strong compunctious visitings of conscience caused by his sin.

The critical event of his life was now drawing near, in his complete conversion and devotion to a religious life. He went to Simplicianus, an old Christian, whom he calls the father of Ambrose,—and to him he explained his spiritual state. Simplicianus related the account of the conversion of Victorinus, a Roman rhetorician, and a very learned man, skilled in the liberal sciences, and who had read and weighed the works of many philosophers. In his old age he was converted to Christianity, at first in secret. One day, he said privately to Simplicianus, "Know that I am already a Christian." Simplicianus answered, "I shall not believe it, nor rank you among Christians, till I see you in the Church of Christ." But he, smiling, said, "Do walls make Christians?"

This kind of dialogue was frequently repeated between them; for Victorinus feared to offend his friends—men of rank and dignity—and he dreaded the loss of reputation. But, after some further study of the Scriptures, and prayer, he said suddenly and unexpectedly to Simplicianus, "Let us go to church; I wish to be made a Christian." When the time came for formally making his profession, he was asked whether he would not rather wish to do so privately. Victorinus declared that he would not shrink from a public profession. Accordingly, he stood, as the catechumens were wont to do, in an elevated place, and, in the sight of the assembled faithful, pronounced, with a clear and distinct voice, the form of words appointed. As he appeared, there was a low murmur of "Victorinus! Victorinus!" for he was well known to them all; and then a silence, as he began the words. The Church, as might be anticipated, was greatly delighted and edified with such a spectacle.

Augustine was fired by so brilliant an example of one of his own country—Victorinus was an African—and profession; but the flesh still lusted against the spirit, and the spirit against the flesh. He even prayed to be quit of his sin, but with a mental reservation; answering, as it were, to the divine call through his conscience, "Presently, presently;" "Leave me a little;" "Convert me, but not yet." But he could not rest; amid increasing anxiety, he was doing his daily work, in the intervals of which he sought relief in religious services. "I attended," he confesses, "Thy church, whenever free from the burden of business under which I groaned;" but he could find no rest even there. The sanctuary itself is no sanctuary to one sinning against light and conscience; he must take the decisive step in order to find peace.

We need not wonder that apparently very slight impulses produce oftentimes great and unexpected changes. The cliff, undermined by waves and showers, is at length brought down by the mere falling of a boulder; or the pile of combustible material, slowly gathered, is kindled at length into a vast conflagration by a single spark. And so is it also in morals. The impulse which gives the final direction to a soul may in itself be very slight. Thus was it with Augustine: a very trifling circumstance sufficed to lead him to the great, decided change on which, in a sense, his whole future life turned, and with it the whole fortunes of the Church of God.

This circumstance was a call, apparently, of mere friendship, made without any special design. One day, when Nebridius was absent, and Augustine and Alypius were together, an African acquaintance named Pontianus, a person of consideration about the emperor's court, called to see them. While the friends were conversing on ordinary topics, a book, lying on a table set for some game, caught the eye of Pontianus, who casually took it up, expecting to find some treatise on rhetoric. It was the Epistles of St. Paul. Pontianus, who was an earnest Christian, expressed his surprise and joy at finding such a book in the possession of Augustine. The latter informed him that for some time past he had studied the Scriptures. The conversation then took a turn; and Augustine heard, for the first time, of Anthony, the Egyptian monk, who, going into a church accidentally, and hearing the words of Scripture, "Go, sell all that thou hast, and give to the poor," took it as a message to himself; and, divesting himself of all property, went to live in the desert. In the course of his narrative, Pontianus related how that himself and three friends, all attendants on the emperor, were walking together. It so happened that, in the course of their walk, they separated into pairs. The other two came accidentally to a cottage, inhabited by some poor Christians: here they chanced to fall in with a Life of Anthony. One of them began to read, and was so impressed, that he determined to retire altogether from court. He said, as he was reading to his friend, "What are we seeking and fighting for, in all these labours of ours? Can our hope rise higher than to be the emperor's favourites? and how very full of trials is this position, even if we attain to it! I will enrol myself as a friend of God. If thou art willing, do the same; but, at any rate, do not oppose me." His friend declared he would cleave to him, "to partake in the glorious reward of so glorious a service." Pontianus and his companion, who had walked in another direction, came in search of their two friends, and reminded them that the day was far spent, and that it was time to return. They declared their intention of remaining; and begged them, if they would not join them, not to molest them. Pontianus and his friend could not make up their minds to this, although they left them with regret that they could not share their higher lot.

All the time Pontianus was speaking, Augustine's conscience grievously smote him: he knew he had been living in sin. "What," he declares, "said I not against myself! with what scourges of condemnation lashed I not my soul, that it might follow me, as I was striving to go after Thee!—yet it drew back, refused, but excused not itself." As soon as Pontianus had left, Augustine turned to Alypius, and said: "Why are we allowing this? What is this now which you have heard? The unlearned take heaven by force; and we, with all our learning, without heart, are wallowing—is it not so?—in the filth of sin." Alypius, seeing how deeply he was moved, looked on in silence. Augustine then went into the garden which belonged to the house in which they lodged, in order to be alone; Alypius following him at a little distance. Here he was in great conflict of mind: he knew he ought to break off his sins, and especially those in which he was at that time living;

but, as he says, "They did retard me, so that I hesitated to burst away, shake myself free from them, and spring over whither I was called,—a violent habit saying to me, Thinkest thou that thou canst live without them?"

While he was thus meditating, and in deep distress, he heard the voice of a child, in a neighbouring house, chanting the words over and over again, "Take and read, take and read." This altered the current of his thoughts: he remembered how Anthony had been impressed with the words, "Sell all that thou hast;" and so returning, and hastily taking up the book he had laid down,—which, it will be remembered, was St. Paul's Epistles,—he read; and the first words which met his eye were: "Not in rioting and drunkenness, not in chambering and wantonness, not in strife and envying; . . . and make not provision for the flesh, to fulfil the lusts thereof." This oracle of God —for such he esteemed it—brought peace to his soul: it was the response he wanted; and, as he tells us, he needed to read no more. His friend Alypius was ready to join him; and thus they both went to Monica. She rejoiced exceedingly at the tidings that they had determined to surrender all for Christ, considering that thus her prayers had been answered altogether beyond her hopes.

The greatness of Augustine dates entirely from after his conversion. His deep learning and unusual natural endowments do not seem to have hitherto served him much; for, though he struggled hard, and panted for fame, he was, as he himself confesses, disappointed. The proximate cause no doubt was, that he could not put out his full strength. He was not single-minded: he knew, in the midst of all his struggles for fame, that there was something higher and better than all this. His deeper convictions, therefore, ever held him back. When once, however, the higher motives had entire possession, and his ministry became all in all, then he made rapid progress, and that, too, almost against his will; for his idea at first was to seek religious retirement rather than religious work. Again, though he never became more than bishop of an inconsiderable see, yet he rose, almost against his will, to be the acknowledged leader of the African Church, and even of the Western Church generally.

He now determined to renounce the profession of rhetoric, and devote himself entirely to the Lord's work; but, however enthusiastic he might be, he was careful to think of others as well as himself. He therefore continued to occupy the rhetoric-reader's chair until the autumn vacation afforded a suitable point at which to break off his labours. Moreover, at this time he began to be troubled with a disease of the lungs, which rendered speaking difficult, and demanded rest. He was not sorry to have so valid a reason for giving up a position which had now become, in his mind, questionable; for he doubted whether he ought to promote an art so often perverted to making the worse appear the better cause. Some over-zealous friends advised him to give up at once the "chair of lies;" but though he had himself some qualms, he surely judged rightly in determining to fulfil to the utmost existing engagements with his pupils.

In the retirement which intervened between his baptism and the resignation of his professorship, he spent his time in the study of the Psalms, which he perused with great fervour. The following Easter, he was baptised by Ambrose, in the church at Milan. With him was also baptised his friend Alypius, and his natural son Adeodatus, a youth of great piety and high promise, but early taken. It is said that on this occasion Ambrose composed the *Te Deum.*

He now determined to return to Africa; and accordingly he journeyed with his mother and a Christian friend named Euodius to Ostia, the seaport of Rome. There they remained awhile, to refresh themselves, before taking the long and dangerous voyage—as in those days it was rightly accounted—to Africa. But Monica was now destined for a better home than her native land: her earthly pilgrimage, although at that moment they had no suspicion of it, was rapidly drawing to a close. It happened, while they were at Ostia, that Monica and her son—now doubly hers, both in the flesh and in the spirit—were discoursing of their heavenly hopes; they seemed in spirit already to have reached those glorious pastures where "God feeds Israel." They dwelt upon the entire happiness it would be if, all other sights abstracted and sounds hushed, they could gaze upon HIM, and hear HIS voice, feeling that but one moment of such communion would be itself bliss, the perpetual continuance of it the joy of the Lord. Thus speaking, Monica gazed out of a window on the closing shadows of evening, and a joyful presentiment came upon her that her work was over in this world, and that the haven of her rest drew near. "Son," she said, "for my part, I have no further delight in any thing of this life. What I do here, and wherefore I remain, I know not, seeing that all my hopes are accomplished. One thing I desired,—and that was, to tarry for a while in this life, that I might see thee a Catholic Christian before I died. My God hath done this for me more abundantly than I could ask or think, in that I see thee now despising earthly happiness, and becoming His servant. What, then, do I here?" A few days after this, she suddenly sickened with fever: in the access of the disease, she became one night altogether insensible, and Augustine and his friends hastened to her bedside. After a while, she returned to consciousness, saying, "Where was I?" and then, looking fixedly on the weeping ones around, said, "Here you shall bury your mother." "I," says Augustine, "held my peace, and refrained from weeping." His brother Navigius said something to the effect that he hoped, as a happier lot, that she might be buried among her own people. She looked anxiously at him, "checking him with her eyes that he savoured such things," and, turning to Augustine, said, "See what he says;" and then, after the pause of a moment, to both of them: "Lay this body any where; do you have no care about that. All I ask you to do is this,—wherever you are, commemorate me at the altar of God." She was then silent, overcome by the severity of the disease. Augustine dwells upon this scene as something remarkable, as indeed it was. Neither he nor his mother was quite free from those superstitions of their times—then comparatively harmless—which were gathering around the sepulchres of the martyrs, to culminate at length in the utterly unscriptural and unprimitive fables of purgatory and saintly protections and invocations. Monica had, during the greater part of her life, expressed considerable anxiety about her place of burial, and had strongly expressed a wish that her bones might, if possible, rest near those of her husband Patricius; for, as she said, they had dearly loved one another in life, and in death would not be divided. But latterly that longing had, through the fulness of the Lord's goodness, begun to cease in her heart; and, in that last memorable conversation in the window, there appeared no desire of dying in her own country. Another day, also, when Augustine was not present, Monica was speaking confidentially to a female friend about the better life, and the blessedness of death. On being asked, "Are you not afraid to leave your body so far from your own city?" she answered: "Nothing is far from God; nor is there any fear lest at the end of the world He should not know where to raise me up." So was she able, in the integrity and singleness of her faith, to rise above those carnal notions which, in one form or another, are so apt to lay hold of the best and holiest of men. In this firm faith, then, that holy and religious soul was freed from the body, departing towards sunrise, on the ninth day of her sickness, in the fifty-sixth year of her age, and the thirty-third of Augustine's.

He closed her eyes, and then there flowed in upon his soul a mighty sorrow, ready to find a vent in tears; but he restrained himself. The boy Adeodatus burst out into a loud lament; but the others checked him: for they did not think it right that such a funeral should be solemnised with tearful laments and sighings, "because they who do this seem to lament either the misery of the departed, or that they are altogether lost; but she was neither unhappy in her death, nor yet altogether dead: of this they were assured on good grounds—the testimony of her good conscience and her faith unfeigned."

Meanwhile, while they whose office it was made ready the corpse for burial, Euodius took up the Psalter, and began to sing,—the whole house joining with the words, "I will sing of mercy and judgment;

unto thee, O Lord, will I sing." Hearing what they were doing, a number of religious men and women came together; and Augustine, taking such as desired it apart, discoursed with apparent calmness upon something fitting for the occasion,—and in touching the hearts of his auditory, he felt a balm to his own bruised spirit. The corpse was carried to the burial, and they went and returned without tears; Augustine sternly repressed all signs of emotion even at the funeral service. He seemed to think there was something carnal as well as natural in his sorrow, and secretly prayed for relief. He tells us, also, that he sought in a bath for a mitigation of the feverishness which his emotion caused, but without effect. At length, sleep came to his relief; and then, awaking, he remembered the hymn of Ambrose:

"Creator, God of all,
  Who rules the turning heaven,
Who decks the day with pleasant light,
  And gentle sleep to night hath given,

That so the tirèd limbs
  For toil may be refreshed;
That so may wearied hearts be eased,
  And carking cares may sink to rest."

Then at last he allowed himself to weep, and confesses that by these "natural tears"—which yet, for one in whom the "sure and certain hope" was so lively, he seems to regard as an exhibition of weakness almost sinful—he was much refreshed.

At this point in his history, the *Confessions* end; and we no further possess, as our source of information, this most touching autobiography.

In consequence of his mother's death, Augustine changed his plans, and returned with his friends to Rome. Here, like his great predecessor St. Paul, he preached the faith which once he destroyed, engaging chiefly in controversy with the Manicheans. Towards the autumn of the year 388, he sailed again to his native Africa. Here he lived, in retirement from the world, at a country house, which he had inherited from his father. He determined now to sell all that he had, and give to the poor, retaining only just sufficient for the moderate support of himself and some friends like-minded, who were, after the manner of the primitive Church, to have all things in common. One of these, who was named Innocentius, had recently been delivered in a remarkable way from a painful disorder. He had already undergone operations more than once, it was hoped successfully; but the painful symptoms returned, and he was informed that he must submit yet again to the knife. His sufferings were so great, and the treatment caused such dreadful agony, that he told his friends he was sure he should die under the operation, if it were attempted. He therefore besought them to come to his house, and pray with him that he might have strength to bear it. They did so, and at length he determined again to submit to be operated on; but great was the joy of himself and his friends to find that their prayers had been wonderfully answered. On the next day, when all was ready, the surgeons found that nature had anticipated them, and there was no need of their art. The friends lived together in prayer, study, and meditation—frequently interrupted, however, by the inhabitants of the city coming to them to take counsel and advice on matters both spiritual and temporal. During this happy period of rest, Augustine wrote several of his most important works.

At the end of three years, he visited Hippo,—a seaport in Numidia, now called Bona,—at the request of a person of consequence. Here he was ordained under somewhat peculiar circumstances. Valerius, the Bishop of Hippo, was preaching a sermon, in which he remarked that the Church needed a presbyter, and that he had frequently prayed the Lord to send him one who could supply his own lack of service, caused by age, and an imperfect acquaintance with Latin,—for he was by birth a Greek. The people, with one consent, desired him to ordain Augustine. Valerius gave thanks that his prayers had been heard, and exhorted him to undertake the office. Augustine, taken by surprise, resisted even to tears, saying that no office was so easy and pleasant as that of a bishop, priest, or deacon, if performed perfunctorily, and with hope of human praise; but, then, nothing was more awful than in such a spirit to undertake it. Feeling, however, that it was a divine call, he was, after a short return to his former retreat, which was spent in meditation and special prayer, ordained by Valerius at Hippo.

His relations with the good old bishop were very pleasant. Valerius showed not the slightest envy of a colleague who was intellectually so much his superior, but allowed the great gifts of Augustine free play for the benefit of the Church, calling on him frequently to preach when he himself was present—a custom till that time unknown in Africa. Here his ministry was especially useful in the instruction and edification of the heathen, and also in the defeat of various heresies; and his fame began to spread gradually throughout the Western World. After a while, Valerius, with the consent of the Bishop of Carthage, made him coadjutor-bishop, that thus, when his own course should be finished, he might preserve to his beloved Church of Hippo the services of one who had proved so able. At the end of three years, Valerius died; and Augustine was now sole Bishop of Hippo, and remained so to the day of his death.

The episcopal residence at Hippo was a model of Christian simplicity and piety. Choosing to remain single himself, although by no means blaming marriage in others, Augustine dwelt with his clergy in common. The diet, furniture, and dwelling were all plain and simple, but good and sufficient; and that there might be no undue preference, no one was allowed to have more than another, not even the bishop himself. He was most anxious that the conversation should be serious and edifying, but above all that there should be no tale-bearing or backbiting. On his table was written a couplet to the following effect:

> "Whoever loves with slanderous word the absent to disgrace,
> Should know that he beside this board can find no welcome place."

Nor did he allow this to be forgotten; for one day, when certain bishops, his intimate friends, were with him, and the conversation took this turn, he remained silent, evidently much disturbed; at length he mildly pointed to the couplet on the table, and told them that he must either have the lines erased, or else leave the table himself. His household thus became a fruitful nursery of worthy ministers,—several bishops, eminent alike for both learning and piety, having been originally members of the clergy-house at Hippo.

He was conscientiously attentive to the wants of the poor, and in times of very severe distress scrupled not to sell the sacred vessels of the Church in order to obtain the means of alleviating it. He set a noble example in respect of offerings and legacies to the Church; he would not receive them, if he thought they were incompatible with the family claims of the donors,—being assured that no blessing would come with property acquired at the expense of those who ought rightfully to possess it. His own moderation we have seen already: what he had was for the Church, and the Church only; he accepted nothing for himself. He voluntarily adopted the single life, abstaining from the society of the other sex with a rigidity which we should think unnecessary, but which, considering what his earlier life was, must be considered an additional proof, if any were needed, of his religious sincerity and earnestness.

As a preacher, he was justly celebrated. His sermons, though in form strange to our modern ideas of what a sermon ought to be, are still justly regarded as a storehouse of very rich material for those who know how to use them. In his explanation of Scripture,—although, as he was but slenderly acquainted with Greek, and not at all with Hebrew, he is not always reliable as an expositor of the sacred words, — he abounds in the development of theological and religious thoughts, even where he evidently misses the natural meaning of the passage, or loses himself, as he sometimes does, in far-fetched allegorical fancies.

The most renowned work of Augustine is the treatise concerning the *City of God.* It was no less than thirteen years in progress; having been begun in A.D. 413, and completed in the seventy-second year of his life. The object of the work is to defend Christianity and the Church in the face of the approaching fall of the old Roman Empire. A strange argument against Christianity had been used. The capture of Rome by Alaric, and the consequent miseries to the empire, had opened the mouths of pagans, who accused Christianity as the cause of the decline. Augustine, in his zeal for the city of his God, gives a genial and noble answer to the calumny. He first of all shows that the downfall of the Roman kingdoms, which was then taking place, was as well a call to repentance to the heathen, as a powerful and salutary discipline to the Christians. He thence turns to the contemplation of the divine kingdom, the city of God, which, founded on the everlasting hills by Christ Himself, can never be destroyed; but, out of all the changes and revolutions of time, must rise again with new power and energy, and, after the fulfilment of her earthly mission, shall—separated even from external communion with the wicked world—enter into the sabbath of eternal rest and spiritual repose.

The other most precious work of Augustine is the *Confessions*, so often referred to already, which forms a kind of autobiography. It is written, as its title indicates, in the form of an address to God; containing a confession of sin, and the methods by which the divine Providence called him to repentance. Its value is very great, because it shows at once his firm and ardent faith, as well as his tender and loving spirit. In style it is, indeed, often over-rhetorical, involved, and interspersed with playing upon words, which sometimes obscures the sense; and, though this was no doubt considered a beauty in a declining age of literature, and so rendered the work specially acceptable to those for whom it was intended, it is really a defect, and one which appears more or less in all Augustine's writings; yet the deep piety and tender pathos which pervade the whole render it impossible to read it without emotion.

The rest of the long life of Augustine is a record of literary labour and ministerial usefulness. His vast influence on religious thought is made manifest by the fact that, though Hippo was but an inconsiderable town, and its bishop likely, under ordinary circumstances, to play but an insignificant part in the affairs of the Church, Augustine was the acknowledged leader of orthodox Christianity in Africa, and even the Western Church generally. But the highest testimony of all to his genius and piety is the estimation in which he is now held. The utmost extremes of modern Christianity, Romanist and Protestant, Ultramontanist and Dissenter, are agreed, if in nothing else, in their veneration of this great father; and thus his reputation survives with undiminished lustre to the present time. Yet, as so constantly may be observed in ecclesiastical history, the immediate effects of his ministry were not destined to have any continuance at all. Ere he died, the clouds of that darkest of all political storms had begun to gather thickly round, and were about to burst on a devoted Christendom, in the fall of the Roman Empire. The Vandal King Gesneric, with 50,000 warriors, had crossed over from Spain to Africa, and had commenced a war which spared neither age nor sex. These barbarians raged like wild beasts, reducing towns and villages to ashes, and carrying torture and desolation every where. They were especially severe against the orthodox clergy,—being themselves Arians. It was therefore a time of deepest distress to the Church, and Augustine's heart was rent with the sufferings. He was not daunted, however, but knew his duty in the awful crisis. He remained with his flock; "for," said he, "whoever flees so that the Church is not deprived of the necessary ministrations, he does what God commands or permits. But whoever so flees that the flock of Christ is left without the nourishment by which it spiritually lives, he is a hireling, who seeth the wolf coming, and fleeth, because he careth not for the sheep." After a while, Boniface, the Roman general, having been worsted by the Vandals, was compelled to retire into Hippo, which was soon invested by the enemy, and closely besieged. All this time Augustine was indefatigable, and preached continually; thus supporting his people under their trials. Daily the conflict grew more serious, and he had to witness one after another of his flock taken by death. His friend Possidonius and other bishops were with him at this trying time; to them he said: "What I pray to God for is, either that He will deliver this city from the enemy; or, if He have determined otherwise, that He will strengthen His servant for his sufferings; or, which I would rather, that He would call me out of this work to Himself." His prayer was granted; at the end of a week from this time, he was seized with a fever, which from the first he hailed as the messenger sent to call him home. He continued his duties notwithstanding, until the extreme pressure of sickness compelled him to retire entirely to his chamber. There he directed the seven Penitential Psalms to be hung up at his bedside, that he might meditate upon them; and desired to be left much alone, that he might, except at certain intervals, give himself wholly to devotion: and in this way he surrendered his soul; sinking to his rest in the seventy-sixth year of his age, after having been presbyter and bishop forty years. His library and writings he bequeathed to the Church. Other property he had none to leave. At the end of fourteen months, Hippo fell, and with it all Africa. But the writings of Augustine escaped the wreck: so that he, being dead, through these yet speaketh.

BERNARD, THE MONK.

Faith amidst the dark Clouds of Medieval Superstition.

"He had imbibed most of the errors of his time which were not directly subversive of the Gospel; and the monastic character—which, according to the spirit of the age, appeared to be his greatest glory—seems much to have eclipsed his real virtues. But if we strip him of this ascetic vest, and consider his interior endowments, he will appear to be no mean or ordinary character."—JOSEPH MILNER.

LIFE OF BERNARD, THE MONK.

IF in the life of Augustine we have a history of a great spirit, who moulded into form the principal doctrines of the Church just at that critical period when the ancient world was on the point of dissolution, and modern civilisation, as we behold it, was about to emerge from the ruin; so in Bernard we have another of those moving minds which give a definite direction to the thought of the age in which they live. There was this, also, in addition, that the period in which Bernard's lot was cast was one of the most eventful in medieval history. He witnessed the first and second Crusades; he beheld, in the rising liberties of the communes, the dawn of that political freedom which we look upon as so happily developed in our own representative institutions. He may be said, in his contests with Abelard, to have felt the first risings of free thought, and assisted, though unconsciously, the development of scholasticism into what was afterward to become modern scientific method. As a monk, he, moreover, represents the spirit of monasticism at its best; as a churchman, he influences the destinies of the Western Church when at the very summit of her power; above all, as a true, earnest Christian, he is, notwithstanding some superstitions incident to his times, a worthy successor of saints before him, and a bright example to such as are desirous of continuing the great work of the reformation of the world.

Bernard was born at Fontaines, in Burgundy, A.D. 1091. His father, Tesselin, was a brave knight, a vassal and friend of the Duke of Burgundy. Notwithstanding his high and undoubted courage, he was of a gentle disposition; but, better than all, he was an earnest Christian. Though a warrior, he was yet a peacemaker; for, having been drawn into a quarrel with an adversary relative to some matter of very considerable importance, the dispute was, according to the custom of those times, to be decided by single combat. The day was fixed, and all was ready,—and, as Tesselin was much the stronger of the two, the chances were very greatly in his favour; but his Christianity enabled him to rise above the prejudices of his age. He felt that such a method of settling a dispute was not in accordance with the principles of the Gospel, and accordingly, before the fight came off, he offered to compromise the matter, proposing such terms as he knew beforehand would be accepted, and thus avoided the strife.

Chaucer's description of a knight—

> "And though that he was worthy, he was wise,
> And of his port as meek as is a maid;
> He never yet no villany ne said
> In all his life, unto no manner wight;
> He was a very perfect, gentle knight"—

might very well have served for Tesselin.

His wife was Alyth, or Elizabeth. According to some of her biographers, she intended to enter a convent, but, at the early age of fifteen, was induced to become the wife of Tesselin. As she was really a devout and earnest woman, it is exceedingly probable that she would greatly wish thus to devote herself to a religious life; for we must remember that, in those days, the monastic life was regarded as the very highest form of Christian devotedness. Called to another lot, she nevertheless spent much of her time in austerities and devotions, which were monastic in all but in name. She was not wanting also in other, and what we should regard as better, evidence of real piety. Active benevolence was joined with personal austerity, and the Lady of Fontaines might often be seen with her own hands ministering in the cottages of her poor and by the bedsides of her sick dependants.

It is especially necessary to observe the form which religious fervour took in that age, if we would estimate aright the character of Bernard. To these rude warriors, religion seemed hardly worthy of the name, unless it partook something of the character of single combat with evil. The shield of faith and the sword of the Spirit must be almost tangible, and wielded according to the rules of a kind of spiritual knighthood. The flesh was to them this visible body of ours; and hence, what method of mortification of it so simple and effectual as to stint it in the matter of food and rest? Medieval Christians, moreover, were taught, equally with their modern successors, that they were to forsake the world; and, again, what more obvious way of doing this was there than to enter a monastery, and so, by a life of devotion, cut oneself off bodily from the snares and temptations of every-day life? and, in the fervour of their piety, men did this. It was a subsequent discovery, forced on the Church by repeated failures and attempted reformations of the monastic rule, that the world, the flesh, and even the devil, could find quite as ready access to souls within the walls of a monastery as on the outside. It is no blot, then, on the character of Bernard or of Alyth, that they practised austerities which we look upon as grotesque or absurd. They could not be expected to rise above their age. It was their method of expressing that fervency of spirit with which they served the Lord.

Nor, again, must we be startled at finding the miraculous largely mingling in their biographies. No doubt the age of Bernard was excessively credulous, and ours, in which a hard, dry scepticism is prevalent, has but little sympathy with it. But it may well be doubted whether the childish faith of the medieval saint, ever ready to discover a miracle where one was not, were not preferable to that cold theology which never recognises the hand of God in human affairs, but would rather speak exclusively of fixed laws of nature. Bernard's age, unlike that in which we live, was always on the look-out for marvellous and sudden interferences in the current of human life. The spirits of good and evil were not only believed to be in contact with our spirits, but often in sensible manifestations to make themselves heard and felt. The root of the matter, which is *faith*, they had,—they realised the divine presence with themselves; but the highest kind of faith they had not: this is seeing Him who is invisible; they craved ever for visible and sensible manifestations of that presence: and their very austerities lent force to the illusion. A man who has fasted and meditated for many hours, is just in the condition to confound inner emotions with external impressions; he will likely enough think he sees visions, as he will most certainly dream dreams. If the reader will bear this in mind, he will be readily able to separate the chaff of fable from the wheat of instruction; and because some things are incredible, he need not fear frauds, either pious or profane, in narratives which were evidently composed in perfect good faith, nor be surprised that such legends could really edify those who heard them.

The circumstances attending the death of Alyth illustrate this fact. She was accustomed to celebrate the feast of St. Ambrose, the patron saint of Fontaines, with great magnificence, on which occasion she always gave a banquet to the clergy. A special revelation was vouchsafed to her, that she should die on the day of the feast. She calmly announced the fact to her assembled household, who utterly refused to believe the prediction. Nevertheless, on the vigil of St. Ambrose, she was attacked with a violent fever, which obliged her to keep her bed on the morrow's festival. She desired to partake of the holy eucharist; after which, feeling strengthened, she insisted that the guests should sit down to the banquet, as usual. After a while, she sent her eldest son, Guido, into the banquet-hall, and told him to summon, so soon as the feast should be ended, all the clergy to her chamber. She informed them with perfect calmness that her hour was come, and asked their prayers. They began the Litany; as they uttered the words, "By Thy cross and passion," she raised her hand to make the sacred sign, and expired. After death, her hand remained fixed in the position she had assumed.

We are also assured that, after her decease, she was wont to appear to her sons; and that she exhorted Bernard especially to continue the good work he had begun, when he resolved to become a monk. But who that knows any thing of the wonderfully vivid images which devoted affection conjures up after years of separation—and Bernard was evidently one of the most affectionate of men—can wonder at all that it should have been so? Alyth's children were wrong in nothing but the desire for visible manifestations of that of which otherwise, in the region of faith, they had most infallible proofs.

To such a nature as Bernard's, then, the monastery was, in those days, the only possible destination. He had certainly two courses open to him: he might be a knight or a monk, and enter upon the career either of a soldier or of a saint; but he was too delicate and fragile for a soldier, and too brave and too earnest to be any thing but a saint. Some of his family thought that something of a compromise might be adopted. He had made rapid progress in the learning of the times, and might thus become a doctor in theology, deeply learned in its hard questions,—victorious, therefore, in those tournaments of intellect, the dialectic contests of the schools. But he determined not to be ensnared with the perilous temptations such a life would produce. The most rigid rules of self-devotion were alone agreeable to his temperament, and hence he determined to become a Cistercian monk.

The abbey of Citeaux had been founded, about fifteen years before, by Stephen Harding, an Englishman, originally from Sherborne, in Dorsetshire. He had introduced a much more severe discipline than at that time prevailed in other monasteries; his object being to restore the rule of Benedict to its original strictness. The luxurious living, therefore, of other monasteries was to be entirely eschewed. The Cistercians were to eat but one meal a day; they had risen twelve hours from their beds, and sung psalms, and worked in the fields, before they got even that one. It consisted of a round of the coarsest bread, and two dishes of different sorts of vegetables, boiled without fat. Their drink was the sour wine of the country, their beer, or a decoction of herbs, called sapa—apparently a kind of vegetable soup; fish and eggs, which were always considered a suitable diet for monks, were rigidly excluded. They were to have but three garments, and those of the coarsest materials. They were bound, as all monks were, by the three vows of obedience, poverty, and chastity. The world was by them to be forsaken, even forgotten.

No sooner had Bernard determined to enter the monastery, than he sought to persuade others to join him. The first convert in his own family was his uncle Galdric, who was a man of consideration and power, and the lord of the castle of Fouillon. His two younger brothers, Bartholomew and Andrew,—the latter having been only just made a knight,—resisted his importunities; but one day Andrew said suddenly to Bernard, "I have seen my mother," who, says his biographer, had appeared to him, and congratulated him on becoming a monk.

With Guido, his eldest brother, he had more difficulty: he was married, and had children, and very naturally—we should say, very properly—objected to leave his wife and daughters. At length he agreed to do so, if his wife would, on her side, give consent. This she refused to do, and Bernard tried in vain to persuade her; but, soon after, she was "visited with a heavy infirmity:" whereupon she sent for Bernard, asked his forgiveness for her obduracy, and became earnest for a religious separation.

The second in age after Guido was Gerard; he treated the matter somewhat lightly, looking upon his brother as an amiable enthusiast. But Bernard, with fiery faith and fraternal charity,—so says his medieval biographer,—addressed him thus: "I know—yes, I know that nothing but tribulation will give thee understanding." And then placing his finger on his side, he said, "The day will come, and come soon, when a lance will pierce this side, and make a way to thy heart for that counsel of salvation thou dost now despise." A few days after, Gerard was surrounded by enemies, and wounded in the very spot where Bernard had put his finger. Being taken prisoner, and expecting nothing but instant death, he cried out, "I am a monk, a Cistercian." In his captivity he sent a messenger to Bernard, entreating him to come and see him. Bernard refused. "I knew and predicted that you would find it hard to kick against the pricks. This wound, however, is not unto death, but unto life." And so it happened; for

Gerard soon after unexpectedly obtained his liberty. He did not—as but too often happens—forget, in his prosperity, vows made in the hour of fear and trial, but immediately joined the Cistercians.

At length, when all arrangements were complete, Bernard and his companions—amounting to some thirty in all—entered the monastery of Citeaux. It will be convenient, at this point, to give the reader an idea of what life in a monastery was like. The following, then, was the ordinary routine of a Cistercian monk's day. At two in the morning, the great bell was rung, and the brethren arose from their beds, and hastened in solemn silence from the dormitory to the church. After a short, silent prayer, they began Matins, which lasted about two hours. The next service, called Lauds, did not commence till dawn; this, therefore, was the time most at the monk's disposal, which he might employ in reading, writing, or meditation—it would vary in length, according to the season. After Lauds, he devoted himself to various religious exercises until nine, when he went forth to work in the fields; at two, he dined; at nightfall, he assembled with the brethren to Vespers; at six or eight o'clock, according to the season, finished the day with Compline; and then went to rest in the dormitory. In summer, when the labours of the field were more onerous, the monks were allowed supper—and then a portion of the day's food was reserved for this meal, but not otherwise. In Lent, as might be expected, the fasts were more severe, and the daily meal later. Rules of silence were rigidly enforced, as well as of strict and unquestioning obedience to the superior. "Put down on paper," says one of its greatest admirers of modern times, "it appears a dead letter of outward observances: the spirit of obedience, humility, and chastity, which actuated the whole, cannot be described in words." This is so. If the great body of the monks were fervent, a little more or less strictness in the rule did not matter; when they ceased to be really in earnest, and worldly-minded men came in amongst them, then it was found that the strictest rule in name was compatible with the utmost indulgence in fact.

At that time, however, there is no doubt that the rule was observed by all with great strictness. Stephen, the abbot, was accustomed to say—and no doubt his rule corresponded with his words—"If you enter here, leave your bodies behind you; let the spirit alone enter: the flesh profiteth nothing." Indeed, to our ideas, such a life appears to contain quite as much of devotion and abstinence as is healthful for either body or soul. But it is an inherent disadvantage in a religion which finds its expression in this way, that it can never go far enough. Bernard, not content with self-denial, went on to well-nigh self-destruction. He so stinted himself in food, that at length he almost lost the sense of taste; the hours devoted to sleep, he looked upon as lost, and passed most of his time in a kind of ecstatic contemplation, insensible to external objects—"a trance, with his eyes open." At length he lost all desire for food, and only ate to prevent himself from fainting; but outraged nature rebelled—these excessive austerities injured his health. Food produced violent pain and nausea; he could scarcely retain any aliment; and what little he did retain, seemed rather to defer death than to sustain life. It is, however, but just to his memory to observe that, in maturer years, he himself condemned these austerities as excessive, and confessed that he had done wrong in thus depriving the Church he served of that bodily strength which was granted him for her and her Master's service.

His ardent spirit by no means allowed him to make sickness an excuse for avoiding his share of the manual labour which devolved on the brethren. Unfit for hard work, he would beg that he might be set to do the most menial offices, that he might make up in humility what he could not give in strength. Stephen also soon discovered how valuable a fellow-helper he possessed in Bernard, and interposed his authority in order to prevent him from undertaking labours which were beyond his strength. Reaping at harvest-time was found to be too laborious, and he too little used to it for him to succeed in performing it. Accordingly, he was enjoined to remain idle while the rest of the brethren were at this labour. He obeyed, but it was a sore trial to him; and he wept and prayed earnestly for strength. From that day, and forward, says his biographer, he became a most expert reaper. The narrative may be believed, without supposing more of a miracle than singleness of purpose is able to accomplish.

Citeaux—which, up to the period of Bernard's arrival, had been but poor and struggling—now began at once to grow in numbers and in usefulness. At first, the strict rule was despised by the careless, and defamed by the self-indulgent. To the earnest and devoted, the strictness and austerity of the rule proved an irresistible attraction. Nay, more; some who originally came as scoffers, only to mock and criticise, remained as brethren. Thus it happened that the little monastery, which hitherto had seen only an occasional novice enter its gates, was now in a position to send out colonies, in order to found other and affiliated abbeys.

But the year of Bernard's novitiate had now passed over, and he was to be fully professed. This ceremony is thus described. The novice was called into the chapter, and before all the brethren made disposal of his worldly goods. His head was shorn, and his hair burnt. Going to the steps of the presbytery, he then read the form of profession, and made the sign of the cross; and, inclining his body, approached the altar. He placed the profession on the right side of it, which he kissed. The abbot, standing at the same side of the altar, removed from it the parchment; while the novice, on his hands and knees, implored pardon, repeating three times the words, "Receive me, O Lord." The whole convent answered with the *Gloria Patri*, and the cantor began the Psalm, "Have mercy upon me, O God;" which was sung by the two choirs alternately. The novice then rose up, prostrated himself at the abbot's feet, and then afterwards at the feet of the prior and all the brethren in succession. Towards the end of the Psalm, the abbot approached with his crosier, and bade him rise; a cowl was blessed, and sprinkled with holy water; and the abbot, removing from the novice his secular garments, replaced them with the monastic dress. The *Credo* was then said; and the novice, now a monk, took his seat with the rest in the choir.

Two colonies had already been sent out; and by the time that Bernard had been a monk a year, a third was to be despatched. Stephen made choice of Bernard as the head of the new community,—he was but twenty-five at the time,—and some marvelled that Stephen should choose so young a man; but Stephen had already gauged the depth and earnestness of Bernard's character.

The ceremony of departure was both simple and touching. They assembled in the church; the abbot then placed a cross in Bernard's hand; he and his twelve monks who were to go with him rose up and bade farewell to the assembled brethren, who on their side responded with psalms and prayers. He then left the church, and the brethren followed him to the gate, and thence on the road, until they reached the limit of their own land; here they parted, amid the regrets of all: for Bernard had, even in this short time, wound himself around their hearts.

Bernard and his monks struck away to the northward. About four miles from La Ferte was a valley with a stream running through it, at that time a wild and desolate place. Here, in this Valley of Wormwood, as it was called, Bernard and his monks took up their abode, and raised up a rude shelter against the approaching winter. It consisted of a single building, which contained both church and dwelling. Its floor was the native earth. The windows were narrow, scarcely wider than a man's hand. Above the refectory was the dormitory, which was reached by a ladder. The monks slept in boxes, or bunks, strewn with chaff and dried leaves. The abbot's cell was at the top of the ladder,—an incommodious little cupboard, with a sloping roof, dark and low; but apparently well ventilated,—for gaps in the woodwork admitted only too readily the blasts of winter and the heat of summer. If this, then, was what the Apostle meant by "enduring hardness as good soldiers of Jesus Christ," Bernard and his monks had ample opportunity to prove their valour.

Indeed, their patience was sorely tried. They had already to subsist on a mixture of beech-leaves and coarse grain, while beech-nuts and roots were to be their food during the winter. Then their clothes and shoes began to wear out; and as the severer weather drew on, the brethren suffered seriously. In their distress, their hopes began to fail. In vain did Bernard dwell with fervour on the higher life, the power of faith, and the love of God,—the half-starved brethren would not listen; and some declared they would remain no longer, but would return to Citeaux. Bernard, seeing that expostulation was useless, betook himself to prayer. A voice was heard from heaven, saying, "Thy prayer is granted thee." "What," said the monks, "didst thou ask the Lord?" "Wait, and ye shall see, O ye of little faith," said Bernard. That day a stranger called, and brought them ten livres. Another day they had no salt. Bernard said to Brother Guibert, "Guibert, my son, saddle the ass, and go to the market and buy some salt." Guibert replied, "Where is the money?" "Believe me," said Bernard, "I do not know the time when I had gold or silver, but HE is above who has my wallet and my treasure in His hand." The other smiled and said, "I shall return as empty-handed as I am going." "Fear not," said Bernard, "but go in confidence; for He who has our treasures, as I said to thee, will be with thee in thy way, and will provide thee all for which I send thee." And so it turned out. Guibert, on his way, met a priest, who asked him whither he was going. He told his questioner of his errand, and the sad state they were in at the monastery; and the priest was so touched with the narrative, that he gave him a bushel of salt, and fifty solidi as well. On his return, Bernard said, "I told thee so. There is nothing so necessary to all Christians as faith." Bernard was right; yet it may be doubted if the expectation of a miracle be the highest kind of faith. After this, we are told that the words of Bernard were held in greater reverence than they had been before. And no wonder; doubtless these trials brought out into relief the best parts of his character, and showed the gentleness of his disposition united to his iron will.

In the mean time, he was solemnly consecrated Abbot of Clairvaux—the "Beautiful Valley," as he called his monastery. His diocesan, the Bishop of Langres,—for in his diocese the monastery was situated,—was accidentally absent; and William, Bishop of Chalons, acted as substitute. This laid the foundation of a friendship which endured through life. William often visited Clairvaux; and the example of the venerable Bishop of Chalons tended much to induce others to enter upon friendly relations with Bernard. So, in abundant offerings, and under the patronage of the good and noble, brighter times soon dawned upon Clairvaux.

But now the infant community seemed to be threatened with a still greater misfortune than it had yet endured. Bernard's health, never strong, worn out by labour and anxiety, began to fail, so that his friend William declares he lost all sense of taste, and was known to have eaten raw blood, which, by mistake, was given him instead of butter; and that he one day drank oil, thinking it to be water: though how such gross mistakes could have been made by his attendants does not appear. At this juncture, William came to visit him, and was justly alarmed at the state of his health. He had, however, the good sense to see what was really required, and obtained authority from Stephen to take the direction of Bernard upon himself. Hitherto Bernard had adhered to the diet and hours of the monastery, as far as practicable; and on being remonstrated with by the brethren, and petitioned to allow himself some indulgence in consideration of his health, he steadily refused. When, however, he was authoritatively put under William, he was as obedient as he had before been refractory. His friend at once enjoined entire cessation from the cares of his office, and commanded that neither his food nor his drink should be regulated by monastic rules. This wise treatment had the desired effect; and by rest and a more nutritious diet was Bernard's health in due time restored.

This wholesome interposition of Stephen's authority was an example of a peculiarity he introduced into his monastic rule. St. Benedict had originally provided for the government of an individual monastery, which was not only to be isolated from the world, but had no necessary relation with any other similar institution. The result of this was, that the monastery depended too exclusively on the personal character of its abbot. A few years under a weak or wicked head would rapidly deteriorate even the best of monasteries, and a high character for piety and earnestness would be lost in utter worldliness. Stephen Harding sought to remedy this by means of a union of all Cistercian monasteries. A general chapter of the abbots of all affiliated monasteries was to meet every September, and to last five days. All must be present; or, in case of illness or other very urgent cause preventing attendance, a substitute must be sent. Over this chapter the Abbot of Citeaux presided; but, great as were his powers,—for to whichever of the affiliated monasteries he came, the abbot abdicated in his favour, so long as he remained there,—he was, nevertheless, only the head in a limited monarchy. The four abbots of La Ferte, Pontigny, Clairvaux, and Morimond could admonish him if he erred; and, if he persisted, could call a chapter of the order, and solemnly depose him. The Abbot of Citeaux was to visit all under him, and these abbots, in their turn, the affiliated monasteries, reporting any deviation from the rules of the order: "so that, if any abbot should be found too lukewarm, or too intent on worldly matters, or in any way reprehensible, he should be accused publicly in the chapter, should ask for pardon, and undergo penance commensurate with the fault." In this way Stephen hoped that the religious spirit would be preserved in perpetuity. It was a vain hope. As the abbeys became rich, they attracted into them, and especially into the highest places, men who were worldly and insincere; and thus these houses of prayer became at length, by the usual process, dens of thieves.

Bernard at this time began his literary labours. His letters are especially valuable, revealing, as they do so completely, the character of the man. In these, genuine humility and Christian love constantly appear; and if sometimes he writes with an earnestness which approaches to harshness, this is but an occasional fault, and must be attributed rather to the prejudices of his age than to any want either of Christian love or of sound judgment in himself. He was a monk with all his soul, and a monastic reformer beside; and he naturally regarded monastic laxity and self-indulgence as the most nauseous of all kinds of religious lukewarmness. A characteristic letter was called forth by the defection of his kinsman Robert, one of the thirty who originally entered the monastery with him, but who was seduced to forsake the austerities of Clairvaux for the milder discipline and more luxurious living of Cluny. It appears that at Cluny a feast-day meant a feast, and a very good one too; while such enormities were allowed as pepper, ginger, and other condiments, and also morning slumbers. Such a defection, especially on the part of a kinsman, was a real trouble to Bernard; and he writes to Robert to expostulate with him,—at that time, indeed, in vain; for Robert remained at Cluny a long time, until Peter the Venerable became abbot, when this really good man,—who truly deserved the name of Venerable,—being essentially a peacemaker, and always ready to do what was kind, sent him back again. Bernard's letter shows that he had no idea of any one being a monk by halves; to him this removal, even to another monastery less ascetic than his own, was a guilty looking back from the plough.

Another instance of the same kind was that of a young man named Fulk. This young man had originally been adopted by a rich uncle, whom he had left in order to become a regular canon. Fulk's uncle, naturally enough, wished his nephew to come back, and eventually succeeded in persuading him to do so. This roused Bernard's indignation; he looked upon it that both Fulk and his uncle were on the high road to perdition, and expostulated with the young man on the heinousness of his offence. Bernard's letter to Fulk is written in a sarcastic strain, and furnishes a marvellous instance of how men are able to blind themselves to what is really just, when led away by zeal in the main praiseworthy. He represents the uncle as saying: "Woe is me! What do I hear? How blighted are my hopes! Is it right, lawful, just, or reasonable, that one whom I have brought up from a child should now, when a man, be the profit of others? My hair is white. Alas, I shall pass the remainder of my life in sorrow, now that the staff of my old age has forsaken me! If my soul were demanded of me this night, whose would my hoarded treasures be?" And then, after a good deal more to the same effect, the uncle is represented as saying: "I will recall him, if I can; even the lad's sense of shame [at forsaking his vocation] had better suffer, than my loneliness should be continued." It never seems to strike Bernard that Fulk might have waited until his uncle, in the course of nature, was taken away; but that, at any rate, till then it was his duty to show piety at home, and requite one who had been to him as a parent. Yet, possibly, it may be a palliation of Bernard's excessive zeal in this behalf, that he felt the old priest's house, notwithstanding his sacred office, was not the place where Fulk would have before him the best example of Christian self-denial and unworldliness.

Bernard was, however, not less strict with those he loved best. One day his sister Humbeline, who was now married, came to the gate of the monastery, attended by a retinue, and in great state, in order to visit her brothers; but not one of them would even come out to speak to her: she was spurned from the gate as a woman who was a sinner. Hurt at her brother's unkindness, she wept, and said meekly: "If I am a sinner, I am one of those for whom Christ died, and have the greater need of my brother's kindly counsel. Command; I am ready to obey." Bernard was moved. He could not separate her from her husband; but he adjured her to renounce her worldly pomp. Humbeline obeyed, devoted herself to prayer and fasting, and at last entered a convent and became a nun. We think it would have been better had he advised her to fulfil her duties as a wife and mother in the world; but he and his contemporaries must be judged by the light that was in them.

We have, of course, in Bernard's biography a plentiful stock of miracles. We have already stated our opinion as to the manner in which they should be regarded by those who would understand aright the history of the middle ages. One or two may be given: they will at least serve to show the esteem in which he was held by his contemporaries. On one occasion, we are told, the flies came into the church in such numbers that the brethren were quite disturbed during their devotions. "I excommunicate them," said Bernard. The next morning, they were all found dead upon the floor of the church, and had to be removed by shovelfuls. On another occasion, Bernard was visiting a friend, and discoursing to her and the company, as his manner was, upon some improving topic. On her lap was her infant of three months old. The child stretched out its hand to grasp that of Bernard, and kissed it with respectful attention.

In the discharge of his duties as Abbot of Clairvaux, Bernard had now reached his thirty-ninth year. At this period, much against his will, he was drawn from his retirement, as simple Abbot of Clairvaux, to become the arbiter of the destinies of the Western Church.

There was a schism in the papacy. Honorius, the pope, was dying; and an anxious expectant of the vacant chair was Peter Leonis. He had secured a large following amongst the cardinals—his enemies declared, by bribery. Another party, adverse to his claims, had determined that, whoever might be pope, it should not be Leo; they therefore assembled immediately on the death of Honorius, and the same evening proclaimed Cardinal Gregory of St. Angelo as pope, under the name of Innocent II. Not to be outdone, the party of Leo went through the form of election, and proclaimed him pope, under the title of Anacletus II.

There were now two popes, each anathematising the other; but, beside the spiritual weapons of excommunication, they had recourse to more carnal and worldly methods of adjusting their claims, and Rome speedily became filled with contending factions. Innocent's party was worsted; and he was glad to escape to Pisa, and thence sailed to France. The northern nations principally espoused the cause of Innocent. The Abbot of Cluny sent sixty horses, loaded with every thing a pope could want, to conduct him to the monastery. This recognition of his claims was all the more valuable to Innocent, as Anacletus had been a monk of Cluny. While there, the pope consecrated the new church,—a most magnificent structure, the wonder of its age,—remaining at the monastery eleven days. All the French abbots and bishops were not equally decided as to the claims of the rival popes, and the necessity for action in the matter became pressing. A schism in the papacy meant, in those days, that in most abbeys two abbots, and in most dioceses two bishops, were contending for the mastery,—one side favouring Innocent, and the other Anacletus,—each anathematising the other. A council was therefore called by Louis at Etampes. To this council Bernard was summoned in an especial manner, and the whole matter referred to him as "a man of God." After fasting and prayer, Bernard gave his decision, which was listened to by the council as though it were the voice of the Holy Spirit. He declared unhesitatingly in favour of Innocent.

Innocent, on this, made a progress through France; and many monasteries enjoyed the high, but somewhat costly, honour of entertaining the pope. Clairvaux was not forgotten. Here he was met by a tattered flock of Christ's poor; the monks followed in procession, preceded by a cross, with downcast looks, and without noise or tumult. Innocent marvelled at the wonderful self-restraint they put upon themselves during his visit: there were no curious gazings, no pushing one before another,—nothing but silent earnestness; above all, the hardness of their fare—this abstinence seemed most wonderful of all. With this abstemiousness it seems probable that their visitors were more edified than pleased. They were certainly not very sumptuously entertained; for only the pope had fish, if there was any. The stay of Innocent here was but short; and no wonder!

Innocent visited Cluny a second time, where, as we have seen, the fare was considerably better than at Clairvaux, and no doubt it was a much pleasanter place for visitors. Nevertheless, Citeaux was not forgotten. Innocent, by a letter from Cluny bearing date February 18, 1132, granted considerable immunities to the Cistercians—amongst others, freedom from episcopal control, and also from tithe. As Cluny held tithes payable by some of the Cistercian monasteries, this was felt to be somewhat an act of favouritism; and Peter and his monks remonstrated, but without obtaining any redress. Peter, however, was, even under this provocation from a rival monastery, true to his character—he would not quarrel; and though in medieval times these exemptions were fruitful causes of the bitterest disputes, it did not destroy the friendship which subsisted between himself and Bernard.

Bernard, besides his vast influence as a man, was most successful as a preacher. At the command of the pope and others, he preached before various audiences; but, whatever his audience, high or low, rich or poor, he was wont to make a great impression. At some of his sermons, marvellous instances of conversion were witnessed: men of high station and great wealth gave up all, and voluntarily embraced the privations of Clairvaux. But all this success in that which was his special vocation, as well as the estimation he was held in by popes and princes, did not destroy that Christian humility which was one of his most striking characteristics. He steadily refused any higher office than that which he held as head of his own monastery; and, though he could make and unmake bishops, and even popes,—though he was admitted to courts and palaces,—he would never be more himself than simple Abbot of Clairvaux.

To his beloved monks, after these intervals of labour on behalf of the Church, he ever returned with affectionate regard; to him, Clairvaux was always the haven of his rest. Here, if any where, he enjoyed peace; but even here he was not without trials. His brother Gerard died. The ceremonies with which the Cistercians surrounded the departure of a brother to the world of spirits were solemn and affecting. When one of the community was very ill, the bell was rung, and the brethren assembled as speedily as possible in the choir. They then went in procession into the infirmary, where extreme unction and the eucharist were administered. When his end appeared to draw near, the dying monk was placed on a serge cloth, under which ashes, which had been previously blessed, were strewn in the form of a cross, together with some straw, or other soft material. The bell was then rung four times, and the whole community hastened to the infirmary. There they knelt around their dying brother, and responded to the prayers which were said by the abbot. Commonly, he sunk away to his rest amid the prayers of his brethren; if life still lingered, the monks retired, leaving a lighted candle, a cross, and holy water.

It was thus Gerard died. Bernard, unmoved apparently, performed the funeral service, while the others could not restrain their weeping. He then mounted the pulpit, and essayed to preach them an ordinary sermon, taking his text from the Canticles—the next in a series of sermons on this book to his monks; but here his spirit failed: he could not keep away from the subject which was nearest to his heart; and, leaving scriptural explanation for the time, he broke forth into touching and eloquent laments, speaking of their and his deep loss. We love him the more for it. It showed that the man and the brother were not altogether swallowed up in the monk and the abbot, and that his austerity and self-restraint arose from earnestness, and not from want of feeling.

Again Bernard was called from his cell to defend the orthodox faith—this time against heresy, as before against schism.

Peter Abelard, his opponent on this occasion, was born in Brittany, in the year 1079. He was a man of great genius, industry, and learning, a renowned disputant in the schools, and well acquainted with the sciences then held in so great estimation, viz. grammar, rhetoric, and dialectics. His opinion of himself was quite equal to that which his companions held of him, which was, however, deservedly high. Not content with the human sciences, he determined to devote himself to the study of theology, which he regarded in the light of a science. Scripture, he declared, was easily mastered by any one of common sense. "Give me," said he on one occasion to his scholars, "any book you please, and allow me a single commentator, and I am ready to expound it." The Book of Ezekiel, as being one of the most difficult, was mentioned. He studied it that night; and the next morning declared his readiness to expound it: "For it is not by leisure, but by energy of genius," said he, "that I undertake to master the sciences;" and accordingly he lectured on it to the admiration of his audience. With Abelard, however, Scripture was but a science, and not a rule of life. His moral character will not bear inspection. We must draw a veil over the story of his wickedness, and the revolting details of the retribution which came upon him. It is not at all wonderful that the writings of such a man should be received with suspicion. Much of what he taught was what the Church in all ages has condemned as false and pernicious; and even the maxims of free inquiry, in which we might possibly concur, would be looked upon with especial disfavour in an age when authority was paramount, and men had not learned to think for themselves. It was, indeed, the first breaking out of that controversy which rages so fiercely in our own times, and which has wrought so much both of good and evil in the Church, namely, that which concerns the relative claims of faith and reason. Had, then, the speculations of Abelard come in a far less questionable shape than they did, hardly any other treatment could be expected for them than authoritative suppression.

Indeed, Abelard had already been condemned by the Council of Soissons before he came into contact with Bernard at all. He had been charged with Tritheism, and with having asserted that God the Father was alone almighty. He was ordered to burn his volumes, and recite the Athanasian Creed. He complied; and, after a short confinement, was set at liberty. It was seventeen years after this, A.D. 1139, that William, Abbot of St. Thierry, wrote to Bernard, entreating him to defend the Christian faith against the alarming progress of Abelard's errors. At the same time, he sent him a work entitled the *Theology of Peter Abelard.* Bernard read the book, and returned answer that, after Lent, he should have, as he anticipated, more time, and would then make himself better acquainted with the subject. He did so; and the result was a private meeting with Abelard, at which the questionable doctrines were discussed; and great hopes were entertained that the matter would be amicably settled, and that Abelard would retract. At first he seemed inclined to do so; but, after a little time, he continued to disseminate his principles, which became day by day more widely circulated.

Bernard wrote to Pope Innocent, begging him to interfere. He assured him that both faith and morals were in danger; and intimated that, if Peter Leonis was the roaring lion, Peter Abelard was the devouring dragon. In the same strain he writes to one of the cardinals: "The dragon has been silent many days; but, when he was silent in Britain" (alluding to the Pelagian heresy, which originated in the British Pelagius), "he conceived iniquity in France. The man boasts that he hath infected the court of Rome with the poison of his novelty. . . . May God defend the Church for which Christ died!" Other cardinals and bishops were addressed in similar language.

Abelard now determined, on his side, to act upon the offensive. At the archiepiscopal city of Sens, there was to take place an exhibition of sacred relics to the eyes and adoration of the multitude. King Louis VII., Count Theobald, and a large number of bishops, abbots, and nobles, were to take part in the ceremony, which was to be of unusual solemnity. Abelard challenged Bernard to make good his charge of heresy before this august and solemn assemblage. At first, Bernard hesitated. "I," he said, alluding to his own inexperience in such contests, and the acknowledged skill of his adversary, "was but a youth, and he a man of war from his youth. Besides, I judged it improper to commit the measures of divine faith, which rested on the foundations of eternal truth, to the petty reasonings of the schools. I said that his own writings were sufficient to accuse him; and that it was not my concern, but that of the bishops, to decide concerning his tenets." Abelard was proportionately elated at this hesitation on the part of Bernard, and spoke to his friends as though assured of victory. Bernard, urged on his side by his friends, felt that he ought not to hold back when the cause of truth was at stake; and accordingly he proceeded to Sens.

The first day of the council was occupied by the display and adoration of the sacred relics; on the second, the great intellectual tournament was to take place. The scene was a magnificent one. The king, surrounded by his feudal lords, and the Archbishop of Sens, with his suffragans, were assembled in the church of St. Stephen. Bernard mounted the pulpit, and confronted Abelard, who stood in the centre of the building; a crowd of priests, monks, and warriors standing on either side. Bernard proceeded to read the passages he had marked for explanation and condemnation; but he had hardly begun, when Abelard rose up, and said that he refused to answer, but appealed to Rome, and thereupon left the assembly. All were taken by surprise. Bernard's friends declared that the cause of this sudden determination was, that Abelard knew that his strength had suddenly departed from him—that he could not answer because he felt a horror and darkness come upon him, so that, afflicted with a kind of moral judicial blindness, he was altogether at a loss. Moderns have seen rather, in this appeal, indications of a dexterous party-move. Pope Innocent could hardly feel very angry with one who, before such an audience, supported the claim of the papacy to decide appeals at a time when such a claim was questionable. The council, moreover, was clearly with Bernard. Abelard was, indeed, suffered to go free, out of respect to Rome; but his book was condemned officially by the council; and a letter was drawn up, requesting the pope to mark such opinions with perpetual condemnation, and to visit with condign punishment all who defended them.

A somewhat different turn is given to this proceeding by Abelard's friends. It is said that the assembled prelates adjourned to dinner, at which a good deal was both eaten and drunk. After dinner, Abelard's book was brought in and read; but the audience grew sleepy, and gave only languid attention: some snored, one rested on his elbows, another got a pillow, another slept with his head between his knees. When the reader came upon some "thorn-bush in Peter's field," he said: "Do you condemn this?" Some answered with a drowsy "We condemn it;" others, roused by the sound, clipped the word to its final syllable, and feebly answered, "'emn it."*

Abelard's appeal to the pope met with the usual

* Lat. *Damnamus*, contracted to *'namus*.

delays incident to such matters, and for a long time passed unnoticed. He accordingly proceeded towards Rome, with the intention of personally pressing his claim. On his way thither, he entered the monastery of Cluny. He was suffering both in mind and body, being depressed in spirit and out of health. The good, kind-hearted Peter received the poor, broken-down scholar with his usual benevolence, wrote to the pope in his favour, and sought to console him during his remaining days, which he saw were not likely to be prolonged. The result of Peter's intercession was, that Abelard was suffered to remain in peace at Cluny as a monk. His health now rapidly declined, and he became more than usually afflicted. Peter, with a kindly solicitude, had him transferred to Chalons, as the most salubrious spot in which the monastery had possessions, and there supplied him with books, as a solace to his suffering. "He spent his time there," says Peter, "in prayer and study; and so the Divine Visitor found him, not sleeping, as He does many, but on the watch."

Bernard, it appears, entered upon these contests reluctantly. He was no controversialist by nature, and was, for the most part, when fighting the battles of the Church, kind and peaceable—a fair and courteous antagonist. In the case of Abelard, he at once abandoned all further opposition so soon as the latter professed his adhesion to the doctrines of the Catholic faith. What Bernard desired most was to be left with his monks in peace at Clairvaux, and to seek their edification and his own by earnest prayer and study of the Scriptures. His ideal of a religious life was that of a recluse; but he never realised it. Again he was compelled to go forth from his retirement: Europe was convulsed with the second Crusade.

The aggressive character of Mahometanism could hardly have failed, under any circumstances, and at any period of the world's history, to raise up a strong feeling of antagonism; and the twelfth century was less likely to endure aggression of this kind than most. The fanaticism of the East awoke the fanaticism of the West. A desperate struggle for the possession of the Holy Places ensued, in which Jerusalem was literally trodden down by the contending armies of the Gentiles. At this time, Christians had possession, and the Latin kingdom of Jerusalem was still subsisting; but the fall of Edessa, which indicated that the scale was about to turn, was looked upon as a European calamity, and a just punishment for Christian sins. Our space does not permit us to give even a sketch of this most interesting history, which is, indeed, readily accessible elsewhere; what we have to do is to delineate the character of Bernard.

Louis VII. had been under sentence of excommunication, but now wished to prove the genuineness of his repentance. He could adopt no better method in that day than to head a Crusade. He was celebrating Christmas at Bourges with more than usual splendour.

Godfrey, Bishop of Langres, who had just returned from Edessa, made a speech, in which he detailed to the king and nobles present the terrible sufferings of the Christians at the hands of the Turks. Louis was so worked upon, that he applied to Bernard for advice. He declined, on his own responsibility, to give advice; but sent to consult Pope Eugenius III., who had been a monk of Clairvaux, and thus a spiritual son of Bernard. The pope returned answer, exhorting to the good work of stopping the progress of the infidels; and appointed Bernard to preach the Crusade.

The first meeting had been appointed by the king to take place at Vezelai: here Bernard preached, and with telling power. His noble form and figure emaciated with fasting, his wonderful eloquence, his sweet voice, and, above all, the depth of his own convictions, as he exhorted to love and self-sacrifice, so inspired his audience, that they were no longer masters of themselves. There had been erected for him a wooden pulpit, on the top of a hill, and the people stood around in vast concourse—all able to see, if too far off to hear. As he preached, a murmur arose, which rapidly became a shout, of "Crosses! crosses!" A large sheaf of them was scattered among the crowd; but this did not suffice for the multitudes who desired to enlist in the sacred army. Bernard tore his cowl into shreds of the sacred form, and threw them broadcast. All the time he was in the town, he did nothing else but make crosses for those pressing in to become soldiers of the cross. At Chalons, a similar meeting was held, at which it was proposed to make Bernard commander-in-chief. Bernard, enthusiast though he might be, was too wise to accept an office for which he knew himself wholly incompetent. To him was assigned the more suitable task of preaching the Crusade in North-eastern France and Germany.

During his progress there, the same success attended his preaching as in other parts; but, besides, he is declared by his friends, who were eye-witnesses, to have worked many miracles. Several blind persons are said to have received their sight; and those who saw this expressly tell us in their accounts that they themselves made the necessary investigations, in order to be assured that there was no deception. That they write in perfect good faith is sufficiently evident, and they fully credited such accounts as the following: A little girl, who had never walked, was suddenly healed by imposition of Bernard's hands. Her mother, who brought her, bounded with joy when she saw her little one, for the first time, standing and walking. On another occasion, a man was brought in a wagon, being too sick to walk, and apparently drawing near to his end. Bernard placed his hands upon him, and immediately he was seen by a number of citizens and soldiers to walk without difficulty. It is alleged that as many as thirty-six such cures were performed in a single day. But the most remarkable point of all is, that Bernard seems fully to have believed in his own powers. His friends ascribed this power to his superior sanctity; but Bernard was himself far too humble a Christian to admit such a solution of the marvel. He remarked that, though he could not doubt the truth of these occurrences, he would nevertheless not believe that it was any thing in himself, but rather that he was permitted to do these things for the edification of others. That he was himself deceived, we are compelled to admit; the more so, when we remember that the Crusade in favour of which these miracles were supposed to have been worked, turned out a most disastrous failure. We must, however, entirely acquit him and his friends of any intention to deceive: at that time, all was confidence—as it proved, vain confidence; but the result of the expedition was not then known. The admiration of his friends amounted almost to infatuation; and, certainly, the hurry and excitement of a preaching-tour were not favourable to calm investigation, and would open the door to profitable fraud on the part of those who had, as they averred, been healed by the popular saint.

The Crusade went forth, and a more fatal and fruitless expedition never has been recorded in the history of religious wars. After two or three years of almost uninterrupted disaster, a miserable remnant of survivors returned to relate their misfortunes, and to marvel at their discomfiture. In the interim, Bernard was engaged again in religious controversy: but now thick clouds began to darken round his life.

His old friend Malachy, Archbishop of Armah, visited Clairvaux, on his way to Rome. Nine years before had he come to them on a visit, but this time he was to leave them no more. He had not been at the abbey more than four or five days, when he was seized with a fever. All that skill and care could do was done, and earnest were the prayers of the brethren for the recovery of their guest—but in vain; he continued to grow worse, and at length his end visibly drew near. On the festival of All Saints, he was plainly dying. He called the brethren round his bed, and, looking up into their sorrowful faces, said: "Greatly have I desired to eat of this passover with you; thanks be to God, I have had my desire." Then, placing his hands on each one, he bade them go to rest, for that his hour was not yet come. They went. Towards midnight, the great change took place: as they sang around his bed, he fell asleep—but so quietly and calmly, that none could say when his spirit left him. In him, death was so gentle, had in it so little of the terrible, that sobs and grief were hushed; faith triumphed: and, with a subdued and holy joy, the brethren buried him in their abbey-church.

But now the failure of the Crusade became known; and with the evil tidings came a deeper trial upon Bernard. Men were astonished at the results; it seemed as though the Lord had forsaken His Church, and had allowed the cause of infidelity to triumph. Bernard shared in the dismay. He had had no doubt of the righteousness of the cause; he had prophesied its success; and now it seemed as if this was a prophecy out of his own heart, when he had seen nothing. And then those who had been enthusiastically with him, turned against him. Had he not preached, prophesied, worked even miracles? His name, so popular, was held up to reproach as the author of the mischief. This, however, probably little affected him: what men thought of himself, he cared not; but he had, it may be, given the enemies of the Lord occasion to blaspheme. He could not account for the result, save by attributing it to the sins of those who took part in the expedition; and certainly they were bad enough. He confesses that his own faith was greatly stumbled. Yet we, who live at a distance, can see not only that he was over-confident, and that what he mistook for faith was only presumption, but that the Christian cause was not nearly so good as he imagined it to be, and, further, that the success of the Crusade would really have been detrimental to the cause of true religion. Yet this, no doubt, overshadowed his declining years. "The judgments of the Lord," he says, "are righteous, as every one knows; but this one is an abyss so deep, that I dare to pronounce him blessed whosoever is not stumbled at it."

Beside this trial, Bernard lost many friends,—Sugar, Abbot of St. Denis, died; then Count Theobald; then Eugenius III., his friend and pupil: and he had no wish to survive them. Then, again, his health was failing. The disease in his stomach assumed an aggravated form: he could eat nothing solid; and sleep almost entirely forsook him. Clearly, and he knew it himself, he could not long survive. His friends prayed earnestly for him; and a slight, partial recovery seemed, to his simple faith, an answer to their prayers. But this was transient. His brethren, in the delirium of their grief, prayed the more earnestly that they might not lose him. Nay, they besought him, as though his life were in his own hands, to remain with them yet a little longer. He was, like the Apostle, in a strait: to depart was far better than to remain in the flesh. Which to choose, he knew not: lifting up his dove-like eyes, he said, "The Lord's will be done." And it was done; for he fell asleep.

Such was the account of his friends; but a letter of his own gives us a different, and yet a higher, appreciation, considered in its genuine Christian humility, of the state of mind in which he met the last enemy. "In the midst of these afflictions," alluding to his sickness, he writes to a friend, "that I may hide nothing from you,—I speak as an ordinary person,—the spirit is ready, though the flesh is weak. Pray ye to the Saviour, who willeth not the death of a sinner, that He would not delay my timely exit, but that He would guard it. Fortify with your prayers a poor, unworthy creature, that the enemy, who lies in wait, may find no place where he may fix his tooth, or inflict a wound." Such genuine, unfeigned, and humble faith is the real victory by which death is vanquished.

WESLEY, THE METHODIST.

Faith arousing the slumbering Church.

"This is the only perfection of men: to know themselves imperfect."—Jerome.

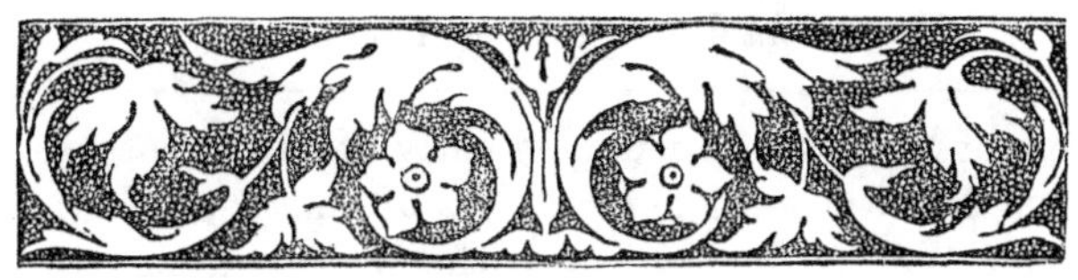

LIFE OF JOHN WESLEY, THE METHODIST.

JOHN WESLEY, the founder of Methodism, was born at Epworth, in Lincolnshire,—a market-town, at that time containing about 2000 inhabitants,—on June 17th, 1703. His father, Samuel Wesley, rector of the parish, was a man of considerable learning and talent. His mother was Susannah, daughter of Dr. Annesley, one of the ejected ministers. Both of them had been brought up Dissenters, but became from conviction members of the Church of England. They had, in all, nineteen children; of whom only six, three boys and three girls, survived to grow up. The names of those who appear in the history of Wesleyanism are Samuel, John, and Charles. The girls were Susannah Mehetabel Martha, Emilia, and Keziah.

It is a remarkable circumstance that the two

founders of Methodism should, in early life, have both been in the utmost danger of an untimely death. The elder Wesley found his parishioners in a profligate state, and zealously discharged his duty in admonishing them of their sins. This caused so much resentment on the side of those who refused to listen, that they determined to set his house on fire. Two attempts were made, both of them unsuccessful; but at the third, they accomplished their diabolical purpose. The family were raised at midnight by falling timbers, and had to escape for their lives. John, who was six years old, and Charles, a feeble infant, were, with three other children, sleeping in the nursery. His father burst into the room, and, awaking the maid, bid her escape; she caught up the infant, and told the rest of the children to follow her: but, in the hurry, John was forgotten, and he slept so soundly that all the noise and confusion did not awake him. When the street-door was burst open, a strong north-east wind drove in the flames, so that, the increased draught adding fury to the fire, in a short time the staircase was burnt away. At that moment, John's voice was heard crying out. The light had awakened him; he imagined it was day, and called to the nurse to take him up. Opening his curtains, he saw streaks of fire upon the top of the room; and, escape by the door being impossible, he climbed upon a chest which stood near the window, in which position he was seen by some who stood in the yard outside. There was no time to procure a ladder, but one man was hoisted upon the shoulders of another, and in this manner he was lifted through the window. Immediately after, the roof fell inwards; had it fallen outwards, they must all have been crushed together. His mother had already escaped by wading through the fire, and was burnt, but only slightly. When John, who was thus the last delivered from the danger, was taken to the house in which his parents were, his father cried out: "Come, neighbours, let us kneel down; let us give thanks to God. He has given me all my eight children: let the house go; I am rich enough." It is in allusion to this circumstance of his early life, that Wesley describes himself as a brand plucked from the burning.

Samuel Wesley, John's elder brother, was eleven years his senior. He had distinguished himself at Westminster School, and afterwards at Christ Church, Oxford, by his classical attainments. He was of sound judgment and good sense; and he so far influenced the destinies of Methodism, that to him, when afterwards an usher in Westminster School, Charles Wesley was sent. John was placed at Charterhouse School, where he appears to have been unmercifully fagged. At that time, the elder boys used to rob the younger ones of their meat; so that John was obliged, for a considerable period, to be content with a small portion of bread only, which served him as his daily food. But this rough treatment neither injured his health nor broke his spirit. He was a diligent and successful scholar. Possibly, indeed, it was one of those hard lessons, early learnt, which contributed to his future success. Thus early inured to privations, he was the better able, in after life, to bear the fatigues and hardships incident to the prosecution of his plans.

While John was at school, an event happened in his family which seemed to border on the supernatural,—this was the occurrence of mysterious groans, knockings, and other strange noises, at the parsonage, which were heard, with the exception of the master of the house himself, by all the family. The elder Wesley, therefore, was as long as possible kept in ignorance of the occurrence, from a superstitious notion that such sounds bode ill to those members of the family to whom they are inaudible. At length the disturbance became so serious, that it could no longer be concealed from him; besides, the noises increased, so as to be heard as loud rumblings, footsteps on the stairs, but, most frequently, knockings about the beds at night. When Mr. Wesley came to hear them, he was inclined to propose strictly natural causes as an explanation of the mystery—he suggested rats or weasels; he hinted that late hours on the part of the young ladies, or even visitors to them, might have something to do with it. This made them hope that he might hear something of the noise himself, and they were speedily gratified; for on the next night, a little after midnight, he was awakened by nine loud and distinct knocks. He rose to see if he could discover the cause, but could find nothing. Thinking it might be something out of doors, he went out, taking a large mastiff with him; but the dog, who had barked at first, now showed the most evident signs of fear, and ever afterwards howled with terror at the sound, and would crouch down for protection near some of the family.

As Mr. Wesley now himself heard the noises, the family had no further fears on his account, but fancied that one of the sons—they fixed especially on Samuel—had met with a violent death. On the next occasion when the sound was heard, Mr. Wesley conjured the apparition to speak, and tell him why it troubled his house. He was answered with three distinct knocks. He questioned it if it were his son Samuel; and if it could not speak, bade it answer by knocking: but no further sound was heard that night. As, in a short time after, the family heard that Samuel, John, and Charles were well, they ceased to be alarmed, and the children would stamp and knock for amusement, when the goblin would reply by knocking in return. Emilia Wesley gave it the name of Old Jeffrey; and, for a while, Old Jeffrey was recognised as a regular inhabitant of the parsonage, until at last he finally disappeared of his own accord. The whole family, as is evident from their letters, were more or less impressed with the supernatural character of their visitor. Thus, one of the sisters remonstrated on the means Mrs. Wesley took to get rid of the annoyance. This was blowing a horn. She had heard that rats could be frightened away by the sound of a horn about the house, and accordingly sent for one. But the goblin resented this horn-blowing, and was more outrageous than ever; and, indeed, generally showed a special dislike to any one proposing, as a cause, rats or any thing natural. Hitherto, he had only been heard at night; but after this, he commenced operations in the day-time. He never went near Mr. Wesley's study, until he called him a deaf and dumb devil; but after that, he became a frequent visitor. These circumstances, and a clue given in a letter of Emilia's, furnish us, we think, with a conjecture as to the true cause of the apparition. She writes to her brother Samuel: "If you should know my opinion of the reason of this, I shall briefly tell you. I believe it to be witchcraft, for these reasons: about a year since, there was a disturbance at a town near us: that was undoubtedly witches; and if so near, why may they not reach us? My father had, for several Sundays before its coming, preached warmly against consulting those that are called cunning men, which our people are given to, and it had a particular spite at my father." Now, all these circumstances appear to point one way. The noises were such as might have been produced, without much difficulty, by some one who had access to the house, as a servant or otherwise, and wished to alarm the inmates. At first, the goblin kept out of the master's way, probably for fear of detection; afterwards, when the family had been sufficiently worked upon, bolder tactics would be both safe and profitable. Naturally, the goblin would be especially angry at any attempt to refer its manifestations to natural means; while a sufficient motive for undertaking this can be found in the hope of profit by those cunning men of whom Emilia writes. Nothing could better serve their purpose than a ghost at the parsonage. If they could beguile—no very difficult matter—the simple, earnest-hearted family at Epworth Parsonage, the rector's sermons would be a source of absolute profit; they would be like an advertisement, and would no doubt promote a brisk trade in the fortune-telling line. When, however, the trick grew stale, and Old Jeffrey was beginning to be in contempt, as a children's plaything, there was equal inducement to continue the matter no further; and then the goblin departs of its own accord. But the family themselves were deeply impressed. Even Samuel Wesley the younger, who was not superstitious, and had by far the most common sense of the party, was not disposed to treat the occurrence lightly; and, as the matter was never satisfactorily cleared up, the elder Wesley, with several of his most intelligent neighbours, both clerical and lay, was satisfied of the supernatural character of the occurrence.

The matter is of importance, as bearing on the early training of the brothers Wesley. It is true that they were absent from home at the time, and so, directly, the excitement caused by the parsonage ghost would have had little influence upon them. But we can understand what kind of early impressions they would imbibe at home. John, in after years, showed considerable credulity in matters where, from his otherwise sound sense and judgment, we might have expected something different. Early impressions may have had something to do with this; at any rate, the continual looking for supernatural manifestations and tokens, rather than an ever-present, superintending Providence, was a habit of mind which modified the system he founded, and has indirectly influenced the current of religious thought even up to the present moment.

At the age of seventeen, Wesley removed from Charterhouse to Christ Church, Oxford. At college he continued his studies with all diligence, and was steady and hard-working. Some of his biographers consider that at this time he fell into a state of religious indifference; but this is probably a too hard judgment: for, when the time arrived for entering holy orders, he began to reflect seriously upon the importance of the ministerial office. He wrote to both his father and mother on the subject for advice, detailing the scruples that he felt. Both answered him as Christian parents should. His father hinted a present delay; his mother advised him to proceed, because she hoped orders might induce him to study still more diligently practical divinity; she wrote, entreating him, in good, earnest resolve, to make religion the business of his life, and to examine himself whether he had a reasonable hope of salvation by Jesus Christ. He took their advice, and diligently prepared himself by prayer, study, and reading. Amongst other books, those which at this time seem to have impressed him most were Thomas à Kempis's *Imitation of Christ*, and Jeremy Taylor's *Holy Living and Dying*. He was ordained deacon in September 1725; and, in the spring of 1726, he was elected fellow of Lincoln College. He now changed his manner of life entirely; he took advantage of his removal to another college to break off with all uncongenial companions, and determined to have no friends but such as truly loved and feared God; he communicated every week, and began to pray earnestly for that personal holiness which Bishop Taylor so strongly urged as necessary to a Christian man. Eight months after his election, he was appointed to be Greek lecturer and moderator of classics in his college,—an appointment which testified no small appreciation of his diligence and powers by the college authorities; in February 1727 he was ordained priest, and became his father's curate in August 1727. He did not long remain so, being recalled by the rector of Lincoln College, in order to take office. On his return to Oxford, he presided as moderator in the disputations—learned exercises, held six times a week in the college-hall. This proved a most useful discipline, sharpening his logical faculties, and giving him great keenness in argument.

His brother Charles had arrived at Oxford before John left: he was a regular and diligent student; but when his brother pressed upon him the necessity for more austere habits, and greater earnestness of devotion, he said that he would not become a saint. While John was away from Oxford, a change came over him, which he ascribed to his mother's prayers. He now, in company with some other undergraduates like-minded, lived by rule, read the Scriptures diligently, prayed often, and went to communion weekly. The usual results followed: Charles and his friends attracted the notice of their young companions by the singularity of their principles and demeanour. To a certain extent this must be inevitable, when any set of earnest men endeavour to live more strictly than those around them; but very possibly they were, after the manner of young men, inclined to glory a little in their singularity, as well as to be zealous in their faith. Accordingly, they were called, in derision, sacramentarians, Bible-bigots, or Bible-moths. Methodist was another and less opprobrious name than these, and, as Charles and his fellows lived by rule, much more suitable. It obtained currency, and, now applied to all who live strictly, whether from good motives or bad, more especially denotes that kind of strictness which Wesley taught.

When John returned to Oxford, the little society gladly placed themselves under his direction. His talents and his university standing naturally commanded respect. The names of the first members were, John Wesley, fellow of Lincoln; Charles Wesley, student of Christ Church; Morgan, commoner of Christ Church; and Kirkman, commoner of Merton. Their object was primarily the study of the Greek Testament; but the society soon extended its operations to other good works besides study of the Scriptures.

Morgan was the most ascetic of the party; his fasts were rigorous. He died early of consumption; and it is possible that his austerities might have shortened his life. But active benevolence was not wanting. He was indefatigable in deeds of charity and benevolence; and what he denied himself, he freely gave to the needy. In these active works the others joined him; and thus they established a custom of visiting the prisoners in Oxford Gaol, and the poor and sick in those parishes where the parochial clergy did not object. Another distinguished member of this society was George Whitefield: he was born at the Bell Inn, in the city of Gloucester, in the year 1714. His father died when he was two years old; but he was carefully and tenderly brought up by his mother, who sent him to the school of St. Mary-le-

Crypt. When he was about ten years old, she married again. This proved an unfortunate step; and, amidst other distresses, his mother's business fell off, entailing on the family straitened circumstances. At this time, his brother used to read aloud Bishop Ken's *Manual for Winchester Scholars.* Soon afterwards, George was chosen to recite one of the speeches delivered at the annual visitation of the Corporation of Gloucester to the school, on which occasion he received the usual present of prize-money given to the speaker on that occasion. With this he purchased for himself the *Manual*, which he diligently studied. He had made some progress in classical learning; but his mother needing help, he assisted her in her business in the public-house, and put on the blue apron, doing all the menial work of a common barman. This continued for about a year, when the inn was given over to a married brother. George still continued his occupation for a while, but could not agree with his sister-in-law, and so left altogether. It happened about this time that a servitor of Pembroke College called on his mother, and told her that, after all expenses of his Oxford course were paid, he had received a penny. "That," said she, "will do for my son;" and, calling to him, she said, "George, will you go to Oxford?" Interest was made without delay, and a servitorship promised. George, on this, returned to school, and, working very diligently, made good progress.

He did not, while at school, neglect to put in practice the lessons of the good bishop, as set forth in the *Manual.* He declares that, before this, he was utterly wicked, even appropriating his mother's moneys from the till to his own use; but now he broke away from all evil courses, prayed and fasted often, and communicated monthly. He was even enabled to promote, by his influence, some reformation among his schoolfellows. At the age of eighteen, he was admitted a servitor of Pembroke College. In those days, servitors actually performed certain menial offices, and were altogether in an inferior social position. This circumstance, which would be equally galling and disadvantageous to most, was an advantage to Whitefield: his skill in domestic duties, learnt in the public-house, led many to seek his services; and, with the income derived from this source, sundry presents, and a loan of 10*l.* to defray the expenses of entering college, he contrived to get through the whole of his Oxford course without incurring debt beyond the amount of 24*l.* His greatest trial was found from his room-mates, who were noisy and riotous, and wished him to adopt their idle and careless mode of life; but he steadily resisted them, remaining for hours alone in the study, benumbed with cold, rather than take part in their vain and frivolous conversation. At length they left him entirely to himself.

He longed greatly to join the society of Wesley and his friends, but was deterred by a feeling of inferiority. At length he obtained an introduction. A woman had attempted suicide; Whitefield sent a message to inform Charles Wesley, in order that he might administer spiritual medicine to her, but desired that his own name might not be mentioned; his messenger, however, revealed his name to Charles Wesley, who, knowing something of his character, asked him next morning to breakfast. Whitefield thus obtained an introduction, joined the little band, and speedily became a leading spirit in it.

They were now about fifteen in number. When they first began to meet, they read divinity only on Sundays, and classics on other evenings; but religion soon became the sole object of the society. They regularly visited the prisons and sick, communicated once a week, and fasted on Wednesdays and Fridays. They also drew up a system of self-examination, to assist them in this duty, and also, by means of prayer and meditation, towards attaining simplicity and the love of God. There was much of real earnestness amongst these young men; but with it was joined a certain singularity of manner and demeanour, which they rather affected than avoided. This not only, as we have already noticed, brought on them the ridicule of the younger members of the university, but also the disapproval of wiser heads, who looked upon their proceedings as likely to lead towards fanaticism and extravagance. But when was zeal, and especially youthful zeal, ever perfectly free from extravagance, or altogether guided by discretion? A trifling incident may supply a wholesome admonition, very necessary for these times. John Wesley would not be at the expense of having his hair dressed, in order, as he said, that the money which would otherwise be employed on this vile fashion might be given to the poor. His mother wrote to him on the subject: she imagined that his long hair was prejudicial to his health, as he was often ill, and advised him to have it shortened; but he declined, on the same grounds of expense. At length the common sense of Samuel hit upon a solution of the difficulty. Could not John have his hair cut so as at once to avoid the singularity of his appearance and, at the same time, economise in dressing? This happy expedient was, it seems, adopted. A more serious matter was the excessive austerities practised by the members, by which the health of several was seriously endangered. Samuel Wesley, on his arrival in Oxford, was shocked to find that Morgan was already far advanced in consumption; his brother John was in such an alarming state, that he spat blood; Whitefield had, on one occasion, so weakened himself with fasting as to be scarcely able to creep. Morgan died early; but John was induced to put himself under proper medical direction, and soon entirely recovered.

His father was now far advanced in years, and exceedingly anxious, upon several grounds, about the succession to the living of Epworth. He knew that, unless he could procure the presentation for one like-minded, his probable successor was not a man who would continue his work. He naturally desired, also, that some provision should be made for his widow and daughters. He urged John, therefore, to take the living, if he could procure it for him. John resolutely declined: he said he was persuaded that he could better cultivate his own soul at Oxford; and determined, in spite of the entreaties of his family, to remain there. Soon afterwards, his father died.

At this time, the trustees of what was then the new colony of Georgia, in North America, wished to send out some clergymen; and, hearing of Wesley and his associates, proposed that some of them should go. At first Wesley peremptorily refused, alleging, as one reason, that he could not bear to leave his widowed mother, who was now dependent on him. When, however, she was applied to, and her consent asked, she answered, like the noble Christian she was, "Had I twenty sons, I should rejoice that they were all so employed, though I should never see them more." After some hesitation, he determined to go. There seemed to open to him a noble prospect of Christian usefulness in the conversion of the heathen. His brother Charles accompanied him: he had, before this, dreaded to take orders, intending to spend his days at Oxford as tutor. Now he was ordained. Their companions were Charles Delamotte and Benjamin Ingham, who was also one of the Oxford society. They embarked at Gravesend, October 14, 1735. On board, they met a party of Germans, twenty-six in number, Moravians, under the charge of David Nitschmann, going out to join a party of their brethren, sent from Herrnhut in the previous year. They were exceedingly impressed with the simple and placid piety of these shipmates; and this acquaintance had, no doubt, considerable influence upon Wesley's religious opinions, and the subsequent discipline of the society he founded.

During their voyage out, they gave their asceticism full play; they abstained from meat and wine, and confined themselves wholly to vegetable food. John Wesley and Delamotte ate bread only, and slept on the floor of their cabins. They were all of them untiring in their exertions for the good of the souls of those who sailed with them, both in public and private ministrations.

At its first arrival in Georgia, it seemed as if the band were to find a successful and edifying opening for their labours; but this was not realised in the result. Wesley was settled at Savannah, where he attained some popularity as a preacher, and an orderly and attentive congregation waited on his ministry; but his success stirred up the hostility of the world. The church was full, and the ball-room empty; and this made some angry. Nor was Wesley careful not to give offence. He is said, perhaps with truth, to have intermeddled in matters with which he had no concern, and so to have occasioned quarrels. He was very strict in carrying out the rubric of the Church of England. He insisted on baptising the infants by immersion, refusing to administer this sacrament at all unless the parents would consent to this form of administration. He would not admit a Dissenter to the communion, unless rebaptised; and refused to bury another, for similar reasons. He divided the church services, having Morning Prayer at one time, and Communion at another. The colonists looked upon these changes as unauthorised novelties; and resented them, as the introduction of a new and strange religion. Possibly these disagreements might soon have been got over; but they were, no doubt, aggravated by a personal incident.

Sophia Causton, the niece of the chief magistrate of Savannah, fixed her eyes on John Wesley. She was a woman of fine person, elegant manners, and cultivated mind; and was introduced to him as an inquirer after the way of eternal life. She adopted the usual feminine arts to ingratiate herself with him; she dressed with great simplicity, became his pupil, and nursed him during an access of fever which seized on him at that time. In his presence, indeed, she was, in sobriety, all that could be desired; but, when away from him, she relapsed at once into the gaieties of the world. On meeting her again, Wesley expostulated with her on this defection. She took his reproof in ill part, and declared her intention of sailing for England. He dissuaded her from this, and they returned together to Savannah. In a short time, she seemed to have recovered all the ground she had lost, and every thing appeared to be progressing satisfactorily. But Wesley's friend, Delamotte, had reason to doubt the young lady's sincerity, and asked him if he meant to marry her. He was startled at this, and evaded a reply, but consulted the Moravian bishop, who replied to the effect that the matter required consideration. Wesley, in doubt how to act, propounded the whole case to the Moravian elders, at a sitting apparently expressly convened for the purpose of deliberating on this matter. They asked him if he would abide by their decision; he answered, that he would. Then said they, "We advise you to proceed no further in this business." He answered, "The will of the Lord be done." After this, he broke off all intimacy with Miss Causton. Entries in his private journal show that this step cost him considerable pain. Soon after this, Miss Causton married a Mr. Williamson; and now her conduct was such, that Wesley thought it his duty to deny her the holy communion. Mr. Williamson resented this, and brought against Wesley an action for defamation of his wife's character; and for a time Wesley was annoyed with vexatious legal proceedings. The upshot of the whole of this most unfortunate business was, that Wesley determined to leave the colony. It is difficult to estimate, at this distance of time, the real amount of blame attaching to either side. Was Miss Causton really attached to Wesley, or only amusing herself with him? His biographers declare that she was set on, by those who disliked his religious zeal, to play the part of a Delilah to this spiritual Samson; but this seems hardly likely. Most probably she liked the man better than his religion, with which she had little real sympathy. He, on his side, seems certainly to have been injudicious. His own judgment of himself at this time was, that he was not converted. He writes thus: "And now it is upwards of two years since I left my native country; but what have I learned myself? Why, what I least expected, that I, who went to America to convert others, was never converted myself."

On his passage to England, he had ample time for self-examination; and the conclusion he came to was, that as yet the great saving change had not passed over himself. "The faith I want," he writes, "is a sure trust and confidence in God that, through the merits of Christ, my sins are forgiven me, and I reconciled to the favour of God;" and this, he says, he had not yet. Nevertheless, his efforts for the spiritual good of those with whom he sailed were unremitting, speaking not only publicly in his ministry, but privately with every individual in the ship. On Wednesday, February 1, 1738, he landed at Deal, passing in sight of an outward-bound ship, on which was

George Whitefield, though neither was aware of the vicinity of the other. Reaching London, he preached on the text, "If any man be in Christ, he is a new creature;" but his doctrine sounded so strange, and appeared so novel, in the ears of a generation accustomed to mere moral essays, that the clergy were afraid, and refused him their pulpits. In London, he met some Moravians,—amongst these was Peter Boehler, a man of powerful mind, and who exercised very great influence over Wesley, and, no doubt, did much towards the formation of his opinions. Charles Wesley had also returned to England, and was now at Oxford. After a time, an urgent message was sent to John, informing him that his brother was dying of pleurisy; he hastened to Oxford, to find that Peter Boehler was there already before him, that the crisis of his brother's disease was over, and Charles recovering. When in Oxford, the singularity of his and Boehler's appearance attracted some attention, provoking ridicule on the part of the undergraduates. Wesley was annoyed at this, especially on behalf of his friend; but Boehler was more philosophical. He said, "My brother, it does not even stick to our clothes." The conversations with Boehler tended still further to the conviction that he was not converted. He even doubted whether he ought not to leave off preaching altogether; but his friend said, "No. Preach faith until you have faith; and then, because you have it, you will preach faith."

At this time, he wrote down the following resolutions:

1. To use absolute openness and unreserve with all he should converse with.

2. To labour after continual seriousness; not wil lingly indulging in any the least levity, or in laughter —no, not for a moment.

3. To speak no word which did not tend to the glory of God, not a tittle of worldly things: others may—nay, must; but what is that to me?

4. To take no pleasure that did not tend to the glory of God; thanking God every moment for all he took, and, therefore, rejecting every sort and degree of it which he felt he could not thank Him in and for.

Now, none can doubt the earnestness of a man who not only made such rules, but attempted, with some success, also to keep them. This real devotion to God's service could have been nothing else than a fruit of the Spirit; yet he was himself, up to a given day, altogether doubtful of his Christian state, and then became so entirely assured of it as to afterwards have no further fears on the subject.

For it was a given day and hour—Wednesday, May 4, 1738. "At five in the morning," he writes, "I opened my [Greek] Testament, at the words: 'There are given unto you exceeding great and precious promises, even that ye should be partakers of the divine nature' (2 Pet. i. 4). Just as I went out again, I opened it on the words, 'Thou art not far from the kingdom of God.' In the afternoon, I was asked to go to St. Paul's: the anthem was, 'Out of the deep' (Ps. cxxx. 1-4). In the evening, I went very unwillingly to a society in Aldersgate Street, where one was reading Luther's Preface to the Epistle to the Romans. About a quarter before nine, while he was describing the change God works in the heart through faith in Christ, I felt my heart strangely warmed; I felt I did trust in Christ alone for salvation: and an assurance was given me that He had taken away my sins, even mine, and saved me from the law of sin and death."

Now that we can look back calmly on the whole events of Wesley's life, and from outside of his peculiar system, we can understand why it was that Wesley should lay so much stress upon the experiences of a single day, and so little on those other evidences of the working of God's Spirit within him which were manifested previously. Wesley's character and early impressions would all tend this way. There is a striking resemblance between him and Bernard; only in Bernard there was a little more of superstition, and a little less of self-confidence: but both expected visible interpositions of God's power, manifest to the eye of sense. Bernard looked continually for direct and visible intimations of divine power, and believed that he himself worked miracles in the world of matter; as that he could restore sight to the blind, and heal the sick. Wesley was, no doubt, better taught; nevertheless, he too was continually on the look-out for special providences, and believed not only that the world of spirits was in contact with this world, but, as in the case of his own household goblin, might very easily trespass upon it. He thus came to overrate the value and significance of religious emotion. He held, in common with all Christian men, that a great change takes place in the soul when it passes from darkness to light, and from the power of Satan to God. But he held, also, that the man in whom this change had taken place must himself be at once fully conscious of the fact; though this not even all his own followers could be persuaded to admit: some declaring that they knew they had been enlightened —but so gradually, that they could not say exactly when. He was self-confident; and also, when once he had made up his mind, was little troubled with doubts or regrets afterwards, but acted on his determination, whatever it might be. Now, all this would naturally cause him to underrate that early teaching of the Divine Spirit which had led him all his life through, and to fasten rather upon some special moment of his religious history when devotion was rising to fever-heat. Such a moment was that from which he dates his conversion. It was at the end of a day of sixteen hours, spent almost entirely in self-inspection, that at length he found the assurance for which he had been seeking; as he says, "Then, for the first time, he saw the Lord." It possibly may have been so; but, even if it were, how came his heart so often to burn within him before? and whence those strivings after holiness in himself, and that desire to see it in others, which moved him to his labours? Because surely his Lord was walking with him, even when his eyes were holden—if, indeed, they were holden; and this crisis, therefore, was rather the moment of enlightenment, than of the first visit of grace to his soul. Unfortunately, however, that which was at best but a personal experience, bid fair to harden almost into an article of faith with himself and his followers, and thus the doctrine of sudden conversion rises into undue importance in his religious system. A proof of this is found in the epitaph of his mother. If ever holy life bore life-long testimony to lively faith, if ever there was an aged widow who came up to the Apostle's qualifications of one who was worthy to be written amongst the Church's roll of her worthies as a widow indeed, Susannah Wesley was such a one; and yet so blinded are men by their own notions, that her sons—who owed to her, humanly speaking, their spiritual as well as their natural birth—chose to date her conversion from a communion at which she ex perienced a peculiar fervour, and described this holy woman's life, up to this point, as a "legal night of seventy years."

Another reason why Wesley should lay so much stress on a sudden conversion was to be found in the general neglect in which the great central truth of the Gospel, the necessity of a change of heart, was practically held. The eighteenth century was really the dark age of vital godliness; and when mankind are spiritually asleep in an age of religious lethargy and coldness, it is no marvel if conversion takes the form of a sudden awakening. It was particularly easy, therefore, at that time, to confound two propositions totally distinct, and to believe that what well-nigh always happened, ought to happen always.

This impression of a great change occurring suddenly, and followed immediately by the full assurance of faith, was still further strengthened by a visit to the Moravian settlement of Herrnhut. It was, indeed, but natural that Wesley should seek to know more of a system which had had so great influence on himself. Our limits forbid us to enter into any details of the peculiar tenets of the Moravian body; but at Herrnhut Wesley found practically displayed that simple, earnest, placid piety,—mixed, possibly, with a little of what we should consider sentimentalism,—so characteristic of the German people. Doctrinally, he and they were at one. One of the United Brethren, for by that name they delighted to call themselves, gave him this definition of the full assurance of faith: "Repose in the blood of Christ; a firm confidence in God, and persuasion of His favour; serene peace, and steadfast tranquillity of mind, with a deliverance from carnal desire, and every outward and inward sin. In a word," he added, as the result of his own experience, "the heart, which before was like a troubled sea, was still, quiet, and in a sweet calm." A blessed experience, truly, if it could be generally realised; but, alas, only a faithful, quiet spirit, here and there, attains to something like it. Yet, after all, no doubt remains that the United Brethren did display a very real and earnest godliness.

"Here," says Wesley, "I would gladly have spent my life; but, my Master calling me to another part of His vineyard, I was constrained to take my leave of this happy place." After a fortnight's stay, he departed on foot, as he came, and returned to England.

On Sept. 17, 1738, he arrived in London. It was still his desire to preach in the churches, but these were generally refused him. Nor was the blame altogether on the side of the clergy. Clearly, the doctrine of assurance, as he and his companions expounded it, would be likely to lead to Antinomianism. Men might trust to this assurance, and cease to lead godly lives; and that this danger was real, subsequent experience has proved. At this time, they waited on the Archbishop of Canterbury; and from this prelate they received nothing but kindness. He affectionately advised them not to give more umbrage than was necessary for their own defence, to forbear exceptional phrases, and to keep to the doctrines of the Church. It was probably at this time that words subsequently quoted by Wesley as occurring in conversation with Archbishop Potter formed part of the admonition: "If you desire," said he, "to be extensively useful, do not spend your strength in contending for or against such things as are of a disputable nature; but in testifying against open, notorious vice, and in promoting real, essential holiness."

Wesley was at this time in no humour to take such advice: "God deliver me, and all that love Him in sincerity, from what the world calls Christian prudence!" He was just in the full fervour of his zeal, and not much disposed to give up any of his own crotchets in order to conciliate. Afterwards, when he waxed stronger and riper in his ministry, he appreciated better the advice of the good archbishop, and speaks gratefully of his kindness. That he was at all times disposed too much to look for visible manifestations, and to overrate the value of religious emotion, is apparent throughout his history; and the accessories of his religious system were likely to promote this.

The principal place of meeting of the society, now gradually taking settled form and organisation, was in Fetter Lane. Here they held their love-feasts: at which they ate bread and drank water in the intervals of praying and singing. "On the first night of the new year," says Wesley, "Messrs. Hall, Kinchin, Ingham, Whitefield, and Hutchins, and my brother

Charles, were present at our love-feast, with about sixty of our brethren. About three in the morning, as we were continuing instant in prayer, the power of God came mightily upon us; insomuch that many cried out with exceeding joy, and many fell to the ground. As soon as we were recovered a little from that awe and amazement at the presence of His majesty, we broke out with one voice, 'We praise Thee, O God; we acknowledge Thee to be the Lord.'" "It was," says the ardent Whitefield, "a Pentecost season indeed; sometimes, whole nights were spent in prayer: and often I have seen them overwhelmed with the divine presence, and cry out: 'Will God indeed dwell with men upon earth? How dreadful is this place! this is no other than the house of God, and the gate of heaven!'"

That the careless and indifferent should scoff at such manifestations was no more than might be expected; and the age, both clerical and lay, was careless and indifferent enough: but many who were thoroughly in earnest were scandalised at the want of discretion and prudence displayed. Accordingly, there were very few amongst the clergy who would admit such men to their pulpits; and most churches were closed against them. This led to the adoption of field-preaching—another startling novelty at that time—which increased the prejudice against them.

At Kingswood, near Bristol, is one of the smaller English coal-fields. Spiritually and morally, the colliers were a neglected race; they were scattered over an extensive district, formerly a royal forest, in clusters of cottages surrounding the pits' mouths. Nominally, Kingswood belonged to the out-parish of St. Philip and St. Jacob; but the colliers, if they had been disposed to traverse the long distances separating them from their parish-church, which was not likely, would hardly have found, amidst the suburban congregation, either space or instruction suited to their need. They were, therefore, just as heathen as were the Indians of Georgia. Whitefield's fervent soul burned within him to minister to these sheep not having a shepherd. He had no church here to preach in; but he was not deterred by this. On Sunday, Feb. 17, 1739, he preached from a mount, in a place called Rose Green. No notice had been given, and only about two hundred were present, who listened to the sermon in something like stolid wonder. But a change speedily took place, and on the next occasion about two thousand were present; and his hearers increased so rapidly, that as many as twenty thousand attended, listening with rapt attention. Whitefield knew how to touch their hearts. As they listened, tears might be seen running down their cheeks, until a white channel was formed in the surrounding sootiness. As the matter then stood, and considering the special circumstances of the case, the ecclesiastical authorities, if they did not see their way to sanction Whitefield's field-preaching, might well have connived; but, unfortunately, those then at the head of affairs could not discern the value of an agency which has since become general; and the Chancellor of Bristol sent for Whitefield, and threatened him with ecclesiastical censure. Whitefield was one of those spirits that would have courted martyrdom, rather than have shunned it; but the days were passed at which a movement of this kind could be opposed by force; and Whitefield was suffered to proceed unmolested.

In the mean time, the cause progressed in London, and with strange manifestations and sudden conversions. Wesley visited a woman who was above measure enraged at the new way, and zealous in opposing it. He argued with her; he besought her to pray with him. In a few minutes, she fell into an extreme agony of mind and body; and soon after cried out, with the utmost earnestness: "Now I know I am forgiven, for Christ's sake." Many other words she uttered to the same effect; witnessing a hope full of immortality. The change, though sudden, was permanent; ever afterwards she continued steadfastly to declare the faith which once she had persecuted.

These kind of ecstasies, or paroxysms,—and the history of all religious movements abounds in them,—have been treated with incredulity, and pronounced to be fraudulent as well as fanatical. But there is no reason whatever to doubt the good faith of Wesley or his followers. They were certainly over-credulous, at this time especially, and over-estimated the value of these outward signs as evidences of conversion. As to the charge of fanaticism, it may well be admitted. Earnest men are apt to be a little fanatical on their favourite topics; and why should religious earnestness be an exception? Far better is it to make too much of religious emotions, than to be without emotion, because there is no religion either.

Whitefield urged Wesley to come to Bristol without delay, and take up the great work, which his return to Georgia forbade himself to prosecute. Wesley hesitated; Charles wished his brother not to go: he had an unaccountable fear that in some way the journey would prove fatal to him. He only desisted from his persuasions when, on opening his Bible, he found the text: "Son of man, behold I take from thee the desire of thine eyes with a stroke; and yet shalt thou not mourn nor weep, neither shall thy tears run down." He looked upon this as a special message to himself, enjoining submission. But the other brethren were not satisfied; and they agreed to cast lots, to determine whether Wesley should go or not. The lot was favourable to his going. They then examined Scripture, to determine what the issue should be, judging by the texts they found; but these were not satisfactory—as, indeed, how should they be? for thus to consult the Bible, is to degrade it to a mere fortune-telling book. We see, however, what great influence chance texts had upon Wesley. He and his friends looked upon it as consulting the oracles of God; but there is no intimation in Scripture that, so consulted, will men find their duty plain, or the concealed future opened to them. But this method of searching Scripture was congenial to that turn of mind which Wesley exhibited throughout—the desire for immediate and sensible manifestations of the divine will.

The fears of the brethren on the part of Wesley proved to be entirely groundless; he was eminently successful at Bristol, and encountered no very serious opposition. But the same kind of paroxysms which had been witnessed in London were displayed amongst his hearers at Bristol, and many sudden conversions took place. Some relapsed again into sin and worldliness; but there can be no doubt that, in numerous instances, the effect was permanent, resulting in a real change of life and conversation, consistently maintained to the end. His brother Samuel, hearing of these things, wrote, with characteristic good sense, to remonstrate; but John answered: "My dear brother, the whole question turns on a matter of fact. You deny that God does work these effects—at least, that He works them in such a manner. I affirm both, because I have heard those facts with my ears, and have seen them with my eyes. I have seen, as far as it can be seen, many persons changed in a moment from the spirit of fear, horror, and despair, to the spirit of hope, joy, and peace; and from sinful desires, till then reigning over them, to a pure desire of doing the will of God." Of course, holding these views, Wesley would encourage, rather than subdue, such exhibitions as the following. As he was preaching in Nicholas Street, almost as soon as he had begun, he was interrupted by the cries of one who was pricked to the heart. Another dropped down on the floor, and then another. A man, by name Thomas Maxfield, fixed his eyes upon a little boy who had thus fallen, and began to roar out, and beat himself against the ground, so that six men could hardly hold him. "I never," writes Wesley, "saw one so torn by the evil one. Meanwhile, others began to cry out to the Saviour of all, so that all the house, and, indeed, all the street, for some space, was in an uproar. But we continued in prayer; and, before ten, the greater part found rest to their souls."

But Wesley, notwithstanding his enthusiasm, was a wise administrator. He was well aware that first fervour, however genuine, will burn out speedily, unless it be fed and tended; and accordingly he introduced at Bristol the discipline which he had found so useful in London, and of which we may conveniently give a sketch here. This discipline was founded on the model of what he had observed amongst the Moravians. Male and female *Bands* were formed, that the members might meet together weekly, under the following regulations: 1. They were to confess their faults one to another, and to pray one for another. 2. These bands were to consist of not fewer than five, or more than ten, persons. 3. Every one was to speak as freely, plainly, and concisely as possible, as to the real state of his heart, temptations, and deliverances. 4. These exercises were to take place on a fixed night in the week, with singing and prayer. 5. Any who were admitted, were asked if they would be open in speech and would conform to the rules. 6. When any member was proposed, the others were to speak freely any objections concerning him. 7. After a short probation, the candidate was to be admitted. 8. There were to be days set apart for intercession and (9) for love-feasts. 10. The penalty for non-observance of the rules was to be a threefold admonition; terminating in expulsion, if the irregularity were persisted in.

Another and important step was the building of a large meeting-house. Wesley, at the advice of his friends, kept the freehold of this building in his own hands: a very prudent measure; as otherwise, if it had been in the hands of trustees, as Wesley at first proposed, they might, if they had become dissatisfied with his doctrine, have ousted him altogether.

For that disagreements of this kind were possible, the experience of Methodism had already made manifest. Hitherto, the Moravians and Methodists in London had formed one body; but the placid Germans were somewhat startled by the vehemence of their English friends, and differences arose between them. In opposing Wesley's errors, the Moravians, as often happens, fell into the opposite extreme, and taught that there are no degrees of faith short of full assurance; and that the way to attain this is to wait for Christ, and not to use means of grace—as private prayer, fasting, communion, or the like. This great divergence on points of doctrine so vital and important led to many conferences and discussions, but all without producing any substantial agreement. These tenets, however, obtained favour amongst the London brethren, so that Wesley, on his return from Bristol, found them greatly estranged from him. He looked upon it that this was a real departure from the faith; and accordingly, having preached one Sunday from the text, "Stand in the way; ask for the old paths," after sermon he read a paper to the following effect: "I believe these assertions to be contrary to the Word of God. I have warned you hereof again and again, and besought you to turn back to the law and to the testimony. I have borne with you long, hoping you would turn; but, as I find you more and more confirmed in the error of your ways, nothing now remains but that I should give you up to God. You that are of the same judgment, follow me." When he had thus spoken, he withdrew—as did eighteen or nineteen members of the society. This breach with his former friends was never healed, although both sides made efforts for a reconciliation. Wesley and his friends moved from Fetter Lane to a meeting-house in Moorfields, which was usually called the Foundry, as it had originally been used as a foundry for cannon.

Another separation also took place. Whitefield had embraced high Calvinistic doctrines of election, and its counterpart, reprobation. Wesley, on the contrary, as the very basis of his system, preached free grace to all. The separation caused considerable pain to both, but it was inevitable. It was utterly opposed to the genius of Methodism—with its love-feasts, classes, and other methods of attracting adherents from the ranks of the world—to damp the ardour of the young converts by insisting that they had no choice in the matter, but that their salvation or perdition was preordained by an irreversible decree. This separation, however, did not destroy the friendship which existed between Whitefield and Wesley, after the first irritation of the controversy had subsided.

Notwithstanding these defections, the cause of Methodism made good progress, and began to take consistent shape; and that not by a code of rules drawn up, but by internal development, determined by apparently trivial circumstances. Wesley had made himself responsible for the expenses attending the erection of the meeting-house at Bristol. Money ran short, and it was necessary to raise more. It was proposed, as a way to meet this difficulty, that every member should contribute a penny a week. It was objected that some were too poor even for this. "Then," said Wesley, "put down eleven of the poorest with me; and if they can give any thing, well, —I will call on them weekly; and if they can give nothing, I will give for them, as well as for myself. And each of you call on eleven of your neighbours weekly, receive what they give, and make up what is wanting." The contribution of class-money thus began; and the same accidental circumstance led to the system of inspection by class-leaders. On calling for the subscription, the leaders sometimes found that some of the members were walking disorderly. Wesley at once saw the use that might be made of this agency; a thorough and intimate knowledge of every member might be secured by an organised plan of regular inspection,—and the leaders were an agency ready to his hand.

The business of leader was to see every person in his class, at least once a week; to inquire how their souls prospered; to reprove, console, or exhort, as occasion might require; and to take charge of any contribution they might be willing to make—either for the poor, or for the expenses incident to conducting the society. In the first instance, the leaders used to visit the members at their own homes; but this proving inconvenient, as many were servants, and the exhortations must be given often in the presence of third parties, not members, the class met together at an appointed place weekly. The leaders, in their turn, met the minister, informed him of any who were sick or disorderly, and paid over their collections to the steward. "It can scarcely be conceived," says Wesley, "what advantages have been reaped from this little prudential regulation. Many now happily experienced that Christian fellowship of which they had not so much as an idea before. They began to bear one another's burdens, and naturally care for one another. Evil men were detected and reproved; they were borne with for a season: if they forsook their sins, we received them gladly; if they obstinately persisted therein, it was openly declared that they were not of us. The rest mourned and prayed for them—and yet rejoiced that, as far as in us lay, the scandal was rolled away from the society."

The practice of itinerancy was also taken up; not from forethought, but as a natural consequence of the course in which Wesley was now engaged. At first it was hoped that the converts which Wesley made would be built up in the faith by the regularly appointed ministrations of the Church; but the extravagance which attended the progress of Methodism had alienated even the more earnest of the clergy, who looked upon these converts with suspicion. Accordingly, there was great danger that they would relapse again into their former state of indifference. What, then, was to be done? Wesley could think of no other expedient than that one "who was upright in heart, and of sound judgment in the things of God," should meet the rest, and inform them in the ways of God, either by reading to them, or by prayer and exhortation. In the capacity of readers, he appointed Cennick to reside at Kingswood, and left Thomas Maxfield in charge in London. From expounding to preaching was an easy step, and it was soon taken. Wesley, who foresaw all the evil such a step would produce, was greatly averse to his converts becoming preachers, and did all he could to prevent it. Seeing the apparent good that was done, he was at length more satisfied, and set himself to control what he could not altogether prevent. With characteristic prudence, he admitted these preachers to serve him as "sons in the Gospel;" but only on the condition that they should labour where he appointed, because otherwise "they would have stood in each other's way." It is quite clear that in doing this Wesley had no idea of separation from the Church of England; nor did he foresee that he had now fairly planted the seeds of a schism. Neither was the blame of the schism which has since occurred wholly on his side. The authorities of the Church of England failed to perceive that an agency had been created which was working to the reform of the lives of a vast number of those who, humanly speaking, would otherwise have remained in ignorance and sin; and that the fanaticism which accompanied it was but an excrescence, which a generous forbearance might soon have purged away.

But the golden opportunity was suffered to pass—not, we trust, never to return.

About this time, Mrs. Wesley died. Wesley was recalled from one of his journeys to find her on the borders of eternity. Three days afterwards, her soul was set at liberty, calmly and without a struggle. He performed her funeral service, speaking on the text: "I saw a great white throne." Wesley has been accused of want of feeling; but this is too hard a judgment,—for that tenderest and most affectionate of sons, Augustine, did the like. But with both of them the motive was the same—an overwhelming sense of the unseen, which taught them not to sorrow as those that have no hope. In the like manner, when refused admission to the pulpit of Epworth, Wesley preached in the churchyard from his father's tomb. He knew that the solemnity of the occasion, and the associations which it would engender, would lend force to his words; and so it proved: his congregation—as well they might—lifted up their voices and wept. The one great object of his life—to save sinners—absorbed all other considerations. His love for his mother was hardly as deep and warm as that of Augustine for Monica; but, had it been deeper, he would have preached all the same.

Soon after his mother's death, there broke out against Methodism some of those popular disturbances so often observed at the rise of a religious movement, and provoked more by its novelty than by any consideration of the real tendency of its doctrines or practices. In many instances, the good sense of the magistrates was able to moderate the violence of the crowd before any mischief was done. Thus, near Epworth, some of the people, in their zeal for the old ways, brought a whole wagon-load of Methodists before a magistrate. He asked, "What have they done wrong?" This was a puzzling question. At length one said: "Why, they pretend to be better than other people; and, besides, they prayed from morning till night." The magistrate asked if they had done nothing else. "Yes, sir," said an old man; "an't please your worship, they conv*a*rted my wife. Till she went among them, she had such a tongue! and now she is as quiet as a lamb." "Carry them back—carry them back," said his worship; "and let them convert all the scolds in the town."

At Bath, Wesley met the celebrated Beau Nash, who came into the room where Wesley was preaching, and demanded by what authority he was preaching there. He answered: "By that of Jesus Christ, conveyed to me by the present Archbishop of Canterbury when he laid hands on me and said, 'Take thou authority to preach the Gospel.'" Nash then affirmed that he was acting contrary to the law. "Besides," said he, "your preaching frightens people out of their wits." "Sir," said Wesley, "did you ever hear me preach?" "No," said the master of the ceremonies. "How, then, can you judge of what you never heard?" Nash answered: "By common report." "Sir," said Wesley, "is not your name Nash? I dare not judge you by common report. I do not think it enough to judge by." When Nash desired to know what the people came there for, one of the congregation cried out: "Let an old woman answer you. You, Mr. Nash, take care of your body; we take care of our souls; and for the food of our souls we come here." Nash found it a very different thing to give the law to a fashionable assembly in the pump-room, and to hold his own in a Methodist meeting; and thought it best to withdraw.

But more serious opposition was in store. At Bristol and in London, the place of meeting was mobbed; and mischief might have ensued, had not the magistrates put down the disturbances with commendable firmness. In all places, however, the magistrates were not so ready to perform their duty; and some were found who, in place of using their authority to keep the peace, even incited the mobs to violence. At Wednesbury, in Staffordshire, Wesley preached without molestation. The colliers of that neighbourhood listened to him patiently; and between three and four hundred persons formed themselves into a society. Mr. Eggington, the clergyman of the town, was at first well pleased with the movement; but offence was given him by some indiscretion; and from that time he opposed the Methodists by the most outrageous means. The magistrates most culpably stirred up the passions of the mobs, when the usual scenes witnessed in such cases followed. Windows were smashed, houses broken open and rifled, men and women assaulted, and some of the latter especially brutally and seriously hurt. These disturbances continued some months. When Wesley arrived at Birmingham, on his way to Newcastle, he came at once, with great courage, to Wednesbury, and preached to a large audience without encountering disturbance of any kind. But, in the evening, the mob beset the house, crying: "We will have the minister! We will have the minister!" Wesley, who never lost his self-possession, desired one of his friends to bring the leader of the mob into his house. The man speedily became calm as Wesley spoke to him, and desired him to bring in one or two more of his most angry companions. The result was the same, and they also became quite calm. Wesley then went out, called for a chair, and, standing on it, said to the mob: "What do any of you want with me?" Some cried out: "We want you to go with us to the justice." Wesley replied: "I will go with all my heart." He then spoke a few serious words—which, as he says, God applied; and upon this the mob cried out: "The gentleman is an honest gentleman; and we will spill our blood in his defence." Wesley asked: "Shall we go to the justice to-night, or in the morning?" The mob answered: "To-night—to-night!" He went, accompanied by a crowd of some 300 persons. On the way it rained heavily. Mr. Lane, the justice, lived two miles from Wednesbury. One or two ran before, to say they had brought Mr. Wesley; but Mr. Lane said: "What have I to do with Mr. Wesley? Carry him back again." In a little while, the main body arrived; but were told that Mr. Lane was in bed. His son, however, came out, and asked what was the matter. One of the mob answered: "Why, and please your worship, they sing psalms all day, and make folk rise out of their beds at five in the morning. And what would your worship advise us to do?" "To go home," said Mr. Lane, "and be quiet." The mob were now at a stand-still; but one advised to go to Justice Peasehouse, at Walsall. All agreed. They hastened on, and arrived about seven o'clock. A message was sent out that the justice was in bed; on which they agreed that the best thing they could do was to go home. Here the matter might have ended; but, on their return, they met a mob from Walsall, and a fight between the two parties commenced, those with Wesley fighting in his defence. But his friends, already weary with their long walk, were outnumbered considerably by the Walsall mob, who carried all before them. For a while, the confusion was too great to admit of his voice being heard; but, after a while, he succeeded in inducing them to give him a hearing. "Are you willing," he cried, "to hear me speak?" Some called out: "No, no; knock his brains out! Down with him! Kill him at once!" Others said: "Nay; but we will hear him first." He asked: "What evil have I done? Which of you have I wronged in word or deed?" He spoke for a quarter of an hour, when his voice suddenly failed; and the crowd began again to vociferate. His voice suddenly came to him again, and he broke out into prayer; when the man who had just before headed the mob against him said: "Sir, I will spend my life for you. Follow me, and not one soul shall touch a hair of your head." Two or three of those with this man then closed round him to protect him; and a gentleman cried out: "For shame! for shame! Let him go." The mob then fell back; and, though the crowd continued, there was no further violence; and Wesley, about ten o'clock, arrived in Wednesbury, with only the loss of a flap of his waistcoat, and a little skin grazed off his hands. At other places, disturbances of the same kind took place. The Methodists were pelted with rotten eggs; and some of the women who attended the meeting were so ill-treated, that they never thoroughly recovered the effects; but, as so constantly happens, these riotous proceedings rather helped than hindered the cause. The preachers, also, who were naturally the objects of this kind of persecution, displayed on every occasion an unflinching courage and fearlessness, which made even their enemies respect them. At length, however, the authorities began to bestir themselves. A few ringleaders were prosecuted; but the Methodists showed a Christian and forbearing spirit, and would not press legal proceedings where they could obtain a promise that the offence should not be renewed; and thus were these riotous disturbances put down.

Methodism had now taken form and organisation. The kingdom was divided into regular circuits, to which preachers were appointed. These preachers met Wesley from time to time in a general gathering called a conference. In due time, legal form was given to this conference by deed of association; and it has now become the well-known body which forms the Methodist parliament or convocation, and by which the business of the society is transacted.

Although Wesley lived many years after these events, there remains very little more to record. He spent his time in consolidating his system, which had now taken root; the work proceeding regularly, without much variation, and the numbers and extent of the society gradually increasing. His time was spent in journeys and preachings, and such-like useful, though in the recording of them monotonous, labours.

Up to middle life, he had remained single; but now he began to think of matrimony. His brother Charles had married a Miss Sarah Gwynne, and settled down as a family-man, contented to perform the duties and enjoy the comforts of domestic life. Possibly the example of his brother, who was forty-one at the time, disposed him to take this step,—at the risk, indeed, of a charge of inconsistency; for he had some time before published *Thoughts on a Single Life*, in which he advised all who were able to receive it to follow the Apostle, and remain single for the kingdom of heaven's sake. The choice he made was unfortunate. The lady was a widow, by name Vizelle, with four children and an independent fortune. Her fortune he settled upon herself, and declined to have any power over it. It was agreed that on no account was the marriage to interfere with his labours; but that he was not to preach one sermon or travel one mile the less because of it. At first, his wife used to travel with him; but her zeal and her affection both speedily burnt out. She became exceedingly jealous of him; and had been known to travel as much as a hundred miles, in order that she might watch from a window to see who was with him in his carriage when he entered a town. She searched his pockets, opened his letters, put his papers into the hands of enemies, in hopes of doing him harm; and even laid violent hands upon him, and tore his hair. She frequently left his house, but, on his earnest entreaty, returned again. At length, when he was on a journey, she seized on some of his papers and journals, which were never returned, and departed, leaving word that she would never live with him again. She survived ten years after this separation, which appears to have been final; and died at Camberwell, and was buried in the churchyard there. Her epitaph declares that she was a woman of exemplary piety, a tender parent, and an attached friend; but is discreetly silent as to her conduct as a wife.

At this period of Wesley's life, when his system was completely matured, it will be convenient to consider the relationship his society had to the Church, of which, to the last, he was an attached member, and from which he was never formally expelled. That a schism might be the result, some had already predicted; and, in the first conference, the question was formally proposed: "Do you not entail a schism on the Church? Is it not probable that your hearers, after your death, will be scattered into all sects and parties, or that they will form themselves into a distinct sect?" The answer was: "We are persuaded that the body of our hearers will, even after our death, remain in the Church, unless they be thrust out. We do, and will do, all we can to prevent those consequences which are supposed to be likely to happen after our death; but we cannot with a good conscience neglect the present opportunity of saving souls while we live, for fear of consequences which may possibly or probably happen after we are dead." In subsequent conferences, the preachers were exhorted to the same effect. They were on no account to allow themselves to be called Dissenters. They were to be preachers, but not ministers; and their chapels were to be called, not meeting-houses, but plain preaching-houses. Yet even then a leaven of ill-will was working against the Church of England, and many of his preachers wished not only to become ministers, but even to celebrate holy communion. This Wesley strenuously resisted. "Lay preaching," says he, "I tolerate, because I conceive there is an absolute necessity for it; inasmuch as, were it not permitted, thousands of souls would perish everlastingly. Yet I do *not* tolerate lay administration, because I do not conceive that there is any such necessity for it, seeing it does not appear that one soul would perish for the want of it."

The reasoning, however, in these passages is more specious than true. Wesley was no doubt doing a great spiritual work, and he was quite right not to be easily deterred from doing it: but then, on the other hand, if it were really a duty to respect the organisation of the Church, not even the sight of perishing souls should have induced him to swerve from it. Even in so great a matter as this, it is not right to do evil that good may come,—and a higher faith would doubtless have done all, and more than all, that Wesley did, without entailing something like a schism on the Church. But every religious movement has its dark side, and Wesley's was no exception. He was credulous to a fault; he was wilfully blind to the real character of some of those manifestations of feeling which did, no doubt, disgrace the earlier history of Methodism. He ascribes the visions, trances, ecstasies, which, in the vehemence of their religious excitement, some of his converts manifested, to spiritual influences, when really they were the result either of overwrought devotion, or, in a few cases, no doubt, of absolute fraud. Nor did he ever get quite clear of this delusion. "The danger *was*," he says, speaking of the earlier period of his work, "to regard extraordinary circumstances too much, such as outcries, visions, convulsions, trances, as if these were essential to the inward work, so that it could not go on without them. Perhaps the danger *is* to regard them too little, to condemn them altogether, to imagine they had nothing of good in them, and were a hindrance to the work." But, say what we will, these visions and ecstasies, which are unlike real prophetic inspiration, in that they are certainly undistinguishable from—some say identical with—mere religious excitement, were a hindrance to the movement; they gave occasion—not altogether unjustly—to the enemies of God to blaspheme. On the other hand, the opponents of Methodism did not observe that which was its real triumph, the certain proof that its conversions were the work of the Spirit,—and this was the amended lives of its followers. Wesley did effect a real religious reformation: and the good results of this were felt in a religious awakening which extended far beyond his own immediate followers. He not only founded Methodism,—a questionable good, and belonging to the dark side of his movement,—but he awoke the Church in England from her stupor. Yet we must not marvel that there is a dark side: when the wheat springs up, then are visible the tares also. Wesley was undoubtedly self-willed and self-sufficient;

however he might deceive himself, love of power was his besetting sin; he was credulous; he was apt unduly to value emotions. In his zeal for the doctrine of free grace, he was in danger of Antinomianism, and his fervour often touched on the border of fanaticism; and so the result was, that the awakening of the Church was accompanied with another breach of apostolical discipline, and another schism of the Church of God. But the Church of England, by her lukewarmness, deserved the chastisement. A higher spirituality on either side would have resulted, no doubt, in a triumph of brotherly love; and Wesleyans would have now been working within, instead of without, the Church of England, to the no small advantage of both. But as things then were, such a union would, after all, have been a doubtful blessing. An accession of strength to a lukewarm Church is only likely to attract into her still more of the worldly spirit than she already displays. Sad as the spectacle is of zeal kept alive by open controversy and schism, it is far preferable to that of a powerful corporation wielding the authority and prerogatives of the Church in the interests of the world. The former is, indeed, unchristian disunion; the latter has a fearful resemblance to the autocracy of Antichrist. The union again of Methodism and the Church of England—which all who love their Saviour, and through Him their brethren, must hope and pray for—will be consummated by an increasing earnestness in both. Peace will be to those who love the Lord Jesus Christ in sincerity, and in proportion to the sincerity of their love.

The life of Wesley was prolonged far beyond the Psalmist's limit of threescore years and ten; and such was his strength of constitution, that the labour and sorrow of the concluding years were in his case but light and easy. One sorrow he necessarily had, which was to see most of his older friends leave the world before him; but, like Moses, his natural force was hardly abated at fourscore years. His face was remarkably fine, his complexion fresh to the last year of his life, his eye quick, keen, and active. He rose every morning at four, and travelled from thirty to seventy miles a day, preaching sometimes as many as five sermons in one day. One of his biographers considers this so marvellous, that he calls it a new thing in the earth. At eighty-five, he had what would probably have been to a young person a slight derangement; but he never quite recovered his full strength. At eighty-six, still further signs of the tottering, declining tabernacle became apparent in weakened sight and stiffening limbs and a decay of memory. He even then did not lay aside his labours, which were, all through life, diligent and earnest, such as very few men indeed have attained to. His last text was: "Seek ye the Lord while He may be found," preached at Leatherhead on February 23, 1791. After this he gradually sank, and died of old age on Tuesday, the 29th, in the eighty-eighth year of his age.

Almost his last words were:

> "I'll praise my Maker while I've breath;
> And when my voice is lost in death,
> Praise shall employ my nobler powers.
> My days of praise shall ne'er be past
> While life and thought and being last,
> Or immortality endures."

And when he could no longer articulate distinctly, the first words repeated over and over again showed the direction of his thoughts. Thus, with the accents of praise lingering on his lips, he departed.

JOHN NEWTON, THE CONVERTED SLAVE-DRIVER.

Faith victorious over blaspheming Atheism.

"Woe to the soul which presumed, if it should depart from Thee, that it should find any thing better. I turned on every side, and all things were hard; and Thou alone wast my rest. And, lo! Thou comest and freest us from our miserable delusions, and placest us in Thy way, and sayest, 'Run, and I will bear you; I will carry you through and bear you still.'"—AUGUSTINE: *Confessions.*

LIFE OF JOHN NEWTON, THE CONVERTED SLAVE-DRIVER.

JOHN NEWTON was born in London, on the 24th of July 1725. His father was master of a ship in the Mediterranean trade; a respectable and good man, but making no special religious profession. His mother was a Dissenter; a pious woman, and member of her Church. She was of weak health, consumptive, and, in consequence, fond of quiet and retirement, which she spent in the endeavour to bring up her boy in the "nurture and admonition of the Lord." John was her only child. Her desire was that he should become a minister; and she hoped, when he should be old enough, to send him to St. Andrew's. But she died early, when he was seven years old: not, however, before the good seed had been effectually sown,—though it was long indeed, and only after many vicissitudes, before it came to maturity.

He was, as a child, a docile and willing scholar;

and had, before he was six years old, learned to read, could repeat all the answers to the questions in the shorter Assembly's Catechism, with the proofs, and all Dr. Watts's Hymns for Children. His father soon married again; but his new mother was of a very different spirit to her he had lost. She was kind to her step-son, but had no deep sense of religious truth; and, after a year or two, the birth of a son so far absorbed her attention, that John was allowed to do pretty much as he liked, and, being permitted to play in the streets, mingled with idle boys, and soon learned their ways. At eight years old, he was sent to a boarding-school in Essex, where he made but slender progress, under the care of a harsh schoolmaster, who seemed to have little appreciation of the natural ability of his pupil; and this was not much mended by an usher, who helped him with his Latin, in which he took considerable interest; but, being ill-grounded and superficial, he soon forgot all he had learned. On his eleventh birthday, he went on board his father's ship, and made with him five voyages to the Mediterranean. His father, who had been brought up in a Jesuit College in Spain, was very strict, and, in his presence, John's appearance was sober and demure enough; but, away from him, he was ready to indulge in all the vices and follies of boys of his age. When he was about fifteen, his father received for him an advantageous offer from a merchant at Alicant, with whom he stayed a little time; but, though he might have done very well had he behaved himself, he soon had to leave, in consequence of misconduct,—only remaining a few months. He would now curse and swear, and was rapidly going down the broad road that leadeth to destruction.

Nevertheless, he could not forget altogether his mother's early lessons; and often had very serious visitations of conscience, during which he determined to break off his evil career. Falling in, when about fifteen, with Barnet's *Christian Oratory*,—although he understood little of its meaning,—he was so struck with the advantage of a religious life, that he began to read the Scriptures, keep a diary, and pray. But he soon wearied in well-doing, and relapsed into a worse and more careless state than before; and yet to wake again. When he was about sixteen, he determined to make a complete reform. He spent the greater part of every day in reading the Scriptures, in meditation, and prayer; he fasted often, even abstaining from all animal food for three months; he would hardly answer a question, for fear of speaking an idle word; he bemoaned his early backslidings very earnestly, even with tears; he endeavoured, as far as his situation admitted it, to renounce society, that he might avoid temptation. And this continued for more than two years. But, as he himself declares, "It was a poor religion; it left me, in many respects, under the power of sin, and, so far as it prevailed, only tended to make me gloomy, stupid, unsociable, and useless." Nevertheless, that it was genuine we cannot doubt; it was an instance of the wonderful working of God's grace in a human soul. It may, indeed, square better with the views of a certain religious system to underrate these first strivings of grace, but we ought to look upon them as examples of those wonderful methods by which God deals with human souls, and draws them to Himself.

But another temptation took him, and again for a while destroyed this hopeful seed: he fell in with *The Characteristics of Shaftesbury*, and read *The Rhapsody* with great diligence, until he knew it almost by heart. This slowly undermined his belief in the very truth of revelation itself. Another advantageous offer was made to him. A Liverpool correspondent of his father offered to send him to Jamaica, and take charge of his future welfare. He was to sail the following week; and, in the interim, he was sent by his father into Kent. Near Chatham resided some distant relatives of his mother, named Catlett, to whom, in her lifetime, she was greatly attached, and in whose house she died. The second marriage of Mr. Newton had caused an estrangement between the families, and they had ceased for some time to hold any communication. John obtained permission to visit the family, who received him most kindly. Mary Catlett, the elder daughter, was only fourteen at the time; but it appears that these children's mothers, as they fondled each other's infants, had dreamed over a project that they should be man and wife. These dreams are seldom realised; but, in this case, a romantic attachment sprang up between them; and, though the visit was only intended to last a day or two, John was so desperately in love, that he could not bear the thoughts of going away to Jamaica, and determined that the ship should sail without him. He stayed three weeks in Kent, until the ship had sailed, and then returned to London. His father was highly displeased, but forgave him; and he now sailed with a friend of his father's to Venice. This voyage he went as a common sailor. His religious principles were not strong enough to resist the bad companionship with which he was surrounded, and he sank gradually back into his former evil habits, though not without convictions and remonstrances of conscience.

About this time, he had a very remarkable dream, which made a great impression upon him. "I imagined," said he, "that I was in the harbour at Venice; it was night, and my watch upon the deck. As I was walking to and fro by myself, a person came to me, and brought me a ring, with an express charge to keep it carefully; assuring me that, while I possessed this ring, I should be successful, but that, if I lost or parted with it, I must expect nothing but misery. I accepted it willingly, not in the least doubting my own care to preserve it, and highly satisfied to have my happiness in my own keeping. While I was engaged in these thoughts, another person came to me, and, observing the ring on my finger, took occasion to ask me some questions concerning it. I readily told him its virtues; and his answer expressed a surprise at my weakness in expecting such effects from a ring. I think he reasoned with me some time upon the impossibility of the thing; and at length urged me, in direct terms, to throw it away. At first I was shocked at the proposal, but his insinuations prevailed. I began to reason and to doubt; and at last plucked it off my finger, and dropped it over the ship's side into the water, which it had no sooner touched than I saw, at the same instant, a terrible fire burst out of the Alps, which appeared at some distance behind the city of Venice. I saw the hills as distinct as if awake, and that they were all in flames. I perceived too late my folly; and my tempter, with an air of insult, informed me that all the mercy God had in reserve for me was comprised in that ring, which I had wilfully thrown away. I understood that I must now go with him to the burning mountains, and that all the flames I saw were kindled on my account. I trembled, and was in great agony; and when I thought myself upon the point of a constrained departure, and stood self-condemned, without plea or hope, suddenly either a third person, or the same who brought me the ring at first (I am not certain which), came to me, and demanded the cause of my grief. I told him the plain cause, confessing that I had ruined myself wilfully, and deserved no pity. He blamed my rashness; and asked if I should be wiser, supposing I had my ring again. I could hardly answer to this, for I thought it was gone beyond recall. I believe, indeed, I had not time to answer, before I saw this unexpected friend go down under the water, just on the spot where I had dropped it; and he soon returned, bringing the ring with him. The moment he came on board, the flames in the mountains were extinguished, and my seducer left me. Then was the prey taken from the hand of the mighty, and the lawful captive delivered. My fears were at an end, and, with joy and gratitude, I approached my kind deliverer, to receive the ring again; but he refused to return it, and spoke to this effect: 'If you should be intrusted with this ring again, you would very soon bring yourself into the same distress. You are not able to keep it; but I will preserve it for you, and, whenever it is needful, will produce it in your behalf.'" The effect of this dream was such, that he could hardly eat, or sleep, or do any thing, for two or three days; but the impression soon wore off, and was in a while totally forgotten.

He returned home in December 1743, and visited Mary Catlett, again staying beyond the appointed time, to the great disappointment of his father. He was impressed, and taken on board the *Harwich* man-of-war. Through his father's influence, he was made a midshipman; and might have obtained promotion, but that he was so unsettled, and behaved so indifferently, as to alienate all his friends. In December 1744, the *Harwich* was in the Downs: the captain gave Newton leave to go on shore; he immediately started off for Chatham, exceeding his leave, and returned to his ship on New-year's Day. The captain was so highly displeased with him, that he showed him no favour afterwards.

His ship, after some rough weather, put in at Plymouth. Hearing that his father was at Torbay, he wished to see him, hoping that he might, through his influence, be able to exchange into some service more to his mind than the long and uncertain voyage to the East Indies. He was sent in a boat to prevent others deserting, and at once deserted himself; but was retaken, and severely punished,—being flogged, and degraded from his rank as midshipman. The captain also showed his displeasure on many occasions, and altogether he was thoroughly miserable; but the worst pang of all was, that he was tortured with the thought that he should never see Mary Catlett again, and, even if he did, he could hardly expect to return in a position such that he should be able to marry her. He had dark thoughts of self-destruction; he even meditated the death of the captain, whom he regarded as his principal enemy; and all this time his conscience was so dead, that he felt no remorse, nor even fear; he became a sceptic, utterly disbelieving in a future state. The only redeeming point in his character was his love for Mary Catlett; for, though now he neither feared God nor regarded man, he could not bear that she should think meanly of him,—and so he was preserved by her memory, as the only light amidst the blackness of despair.

His ship arrived at Madeira; and here he was exchanged into a merchant-vessel, bound for Sierra Leone. The commander happened to know his father, and was disposed to befriend him; but his wayward conduct alienated him, as it had done others. For some fancied slight, he held him up to the ridicule of his crew. The captain, however, died on the coast of Africa, and the mate took the command. With him he was on no better terms. He was afraid, therefore, if he went to the West Indies,—the destination of the ship,—that he should again be exchanged into a man-of-war. To avoid this, he determined to remain on the coast of Africa.

Here he entered into the slave-trade, attracted into it by the success of a man he met on board, who had gained a considerable sum of money by this traffic. He imprudently made no terms with this man, and received nothing but a bill on the owners in England, which, in consequence of their subsequent bankruptcy, was never paid. He thus found himself on the coast of Africa, with little more than the clothes upon his back to call his own. And now, for two years, he was literally and actually in the condition of the prodigal in the parable. The man with whom he was associated, and whom he was obliged to serve in a capacity not at all above that of a slave, was under the influence of a black woman, with whom he lived as his wife. This woman very soon became greatly prejudiced against John Newton. He had fallen sick, and had been at first tended by her with some natural woman's kindness; but, after a little time, she became tired of her charge, and treated him with neglect and contumely. He could not, though parched with fever, obtain sometimes even a drink of water. His bed was a mat spread upon a board or chest, and a log was his pillow. As he got better, his appetite returned, and indeed he suffered dreadfully from hunger; but his mistress, although revelling in plenty, would not allow him sufficient to appease his appetite. When in an unusually good humour, she would send him victuals in her own plate, after she had dined; and so low was he reduced, that he was only too glad to receive them. On one occasion, he dropped the plate from weakness; but, though the table was covered with dishes, she only laughed at him, and refused to let him have more. He was even reduced to eat raw plantains, which he secretly pulled up at night, and which, in their uncooked state, proved very unwholesome. Sometimes even the slaves brought him food secretly,—for they dared not do it openly,—to such a depth had he sunk in want and degradation. On his recovery, he went a voyage with his master. He was falsely accused to him of a theft—the only crime, he says, of which he was never guilty—and was, in consequence, treated like a prisoner. He was not allowed to leave the deck; his food was a pint of rice, and such fish as he was able to catch. It was only during slack tide that fishing was practicable. If lucky enough to catch one, this fish, broiled, or rather half-burnt, without sauce, salt, or bread, served as his meal, which, in his starved condition, he looked upon as delicious; if he failed, he must sleep away his hunger as he best could until the next tide. He had brought ashore with him the only book he possessed, a copy of Euclid's *Elements;* and, during this miserable period, he lost for a while, in the contemplation of lines and angles, the sense of his wretchedness, and in this way made himself master of the first six books.

He lived thus for about a twelvemonth, during which time he wrote several times to his father, describing his abject condition. His father applied to a friend at Liverpool, who gave orders to one of his captains, at that time fitting out for Sierra Leone, to inquire after him.

But now his circumstances began to improve a little: he went to another trader, who treated him much better. To him Newton proved a valuable assistant. The trader gave him a share of the business; and they settled near a river which runs parallel to the coast for many miles, so as to be seldom more than three miles from the sea, and often much nearer. Newton now became so far assimilated to the natives and their mode of life, as to partake in the ceremonies of their heathenism, and even partly to believe in the efficacy of their charms and amulets, becoming almost one of themselves; and, indeed, he might perhaps have become so altogether, had not the memory of Mary Catlett—the good genius of his life—still kept up a lingering connection with European civilisation and faith. He was at this time a profane swearer; and, not content with the ordinary oaths, he would invent novelties in blasphemy, so horrible as to shock the not over-sensitive consciences of his slave-driving companions.

The captain from Liverpool arrived out, and made inquiry for him along the coast, but without success. Newton had gone up the river above mentioned nearly a hundred miles. In consequence of its peculiar formation, he was at no great distance from the coast; and, happening to be in want of some necessaries, went to look out for a passing ship, from which he anticipated that, by means of barter, he would be able to supply himself. A ship passed, saw his signals, and put in. It turned out to be the very ship in search of him; but he was now so prosperous, that he hardly cared to return. The captain of the ship, not wishing to go back without him, told Newton that he had had a legacy of the value of 400*l.* a year bequeathed to him by a relative. This was untrue, being a pure invention on the part of the captain; but Newton was thus induced to return to England, as it opened a prospect to him of marrying Mary Catlett,—although, as he confesses, the sense of duty to his father—who had taken so much pains about him, and had directed no expense to be spared in order to obtain his release—would have been altogether powerless.

During the voyage home, which was a long and disastrous one, and the weather bad, he showed tolerably clearly what sort of person he was. The captain declared that Newton was like a Jonah in the ship, and that all the troubles and disasters he encountered arose from taking him into his vessel. On board the vessel were but few books,—one of them was Stanhope's *Thomas à Kempis.* Newton took this up carelessly, in order to beguile the time; but, as he was reading, the thought one day struck him, what if it were true? He shut the book, for he could not bear the inference; and he closed it for that time with the reflection that, any way, *his* choice was made. But though this was, to all appearance, a passing thought, undistinguishable from other like compunctious visitings, it proved to be in reality the first movings of that divine grace by which he was to be finally rescued from his life of sin.

That night, he was awoke by a heavy sea bursting over the vessel: he rushed up from his berth, to find the ship filling fast, and the upper timbers a complete wreck. They went to work with the pumps; and these proving insufficient to gain upon the leak, the whole crew were set to bailing; and, indeed, had not it been that the cargo was of such specifically light materials as wood and beeswax, the ship must inevitably have sunk. At daybreak the storm abated a little, and they expended most of their clothes and bedding in stopping the leaks.

All this time, Newton was working hard and courageously: he even observed to one of his companions, that in a few days the matter would furnish a subject of conversation over a glass of wine; but his companion, in more serious mood, replied that it was too late now. About nine o'clock in the morning, Newton, almost spent with labour, went to speak to the captain —apparently about performing some nautical manœuvre—and as he was returning, he said, almost without meaning, "If this will not do, the Lord have mercy upon us." The words, however, smote home; he reflected, as he said them, "What mercy is there for me?" He was, however, obliged to return to the pumps; and continued working at them till noon, when he became so exhausted as to be compelled to lie down for about an hour, not knowing, as the ship laboured amidst the waves, and from time to time settled down in the trough of the sea, whether she would ever right herself again. He then got up, and, being too much exhausted to pump, went to the helm to steer, and continued at this work till midnight. Here he had more time for reflection, and began to think of his religious professions and resolutions, followed, as they had been, by his licentious conversation and railings against the Gospel history; and at first it seemed to him as though, thus offending against light and knowledge, he had sinned too deeply to be forgiven. But as the situation of the ship became less precarious, and there seemed some hope that they would be saved, it appeared as though the hand of God was put forth in his favour, and he began to pray.

But he was now the victim of doubts and fears: he rather wished that Christianity were true, than fully believed that it was so; "for," says he, "I began to feel my own sinfulness, and longed to find some way out of it. This the Gospel seemed to promise; but on every other side was I surrounded with black, unfathomable despair."

The next day, the wind went down, and the weather continued fair. The ship's company imagined that they must be about 300 miles from the north-west of Ireland, though in reality the distance was much greater. The damaged part of the vessel had to be kept to windward, if there were the least sea on; and as they had but few sails, and these old and weak, their progress was necessarily very slow. This continued about four or five days, when the watch awoke them one morning with the cry of "Land ahead!" and they fancied they descried the outline of the coast of Ireland, for which they were making. As the morning dawned, the land proved to be but a bank of clouds; and the next day a gale sprang up, which drove them out of their course, towards the western islands of Scotland. Their provisions now began to run short, and they were in great danger of starvation; beside which, the incessant labour at the pumps exhausted their strength; and one of the crew died, in consequence of the hardships from which he suffered. The captain, also, was continually reproaching Newton with being the cause of the calamity. He was confident that the only way to save the ship would be to throw him overboard; and, though he had no real intention of making the experiment, Newton could not but feel that he at least deserved that thus the hand of God should find him out in his wickedness. But the wind changed, and continued unexpectedly fair; and, in a few days, land was really in sight. This proved to be the island of Tory; and the next day, April 8, they anchored in Lough Swilly, but not a day too soon. Their last meal was cooking when they arrived; and, not two hours afterwards, a gale arose, which must, in all probability, had they encountered it, have destroyed their vessel. "But," says Newton, "about this time I began to know that there is a God that hears and answers prayers."

After this crisis in his life, Newton became a reformed character: he entirely gave up the habit of swearing, which had previously seemed almost a second nature; and was no longer an infidel, but was sincerely touched with a sense of the undeserved mercies he had received. That he had still much to learn, is not to be wondered at; but he grew in grace and the knowledge of God. At this time he had no religious friends, but was only occasionally in the society of those who thought seriously; being, for the next six years, almost entirely shut off from the means of grace, still in the midst of his former companions, and exposed to the same evil influence and example as before.

While the ship was refitting at Lough Swilly, Newton proceeded to Londonderry. Here he determined to receive the communion, and prepared himself with great fervency and earnestness for it. Here was another step in his spiritual life; and though this first fervour, which was real and genuine, did not continue, he felt a peace and satisfaction in his holy service to which he had hitherto been a stranger.

While in Ireland, he wrote home. His father, who had no expectation of hearing of him again,—for the vessel in which he sailed had been given up as lost,—was on the point of departure for Hudson's Bay. He had intended to take his son with him on his return to England, but he died at Hudson's Bay; and thus Newton never saw him again. Before he left England, the elder Mr. Newton paid a visit to the Catletts, and gave his consent to his son's marriage with Mary.

Newton arrived in Liverpool just at the time his father sailed from the Nore. Here he met with the gentleman whose ship had brought him home, who behaved with the greatest kindness, and promised him all the assistance in his power,—a promise which he nobly kept. He even offered Newton the command of a ship, which Newton declined at that time, on the ground that he had been hitherto so careless and unsettled, that he had rather not take so responsible a position till he had learned obedience and something more of business: a remarkable instance, truly, of the change which real religion produces in those who are subject to its influence. Hitherto, no arguments nor persuasions, no views of his own interest nor regard to the future, could have restrained him within the bounds even of common prudence; and now he was so humble and diffident of his own powers as to take voluntarily a subordinate position. The mate of the vessel in which he came home was made captain, and he was engaged to go as first mate under him.

Nevertheless, he relaxed a little in his religious life; he became careless, and his conversation light and frivolous, though not profane. He neither prayed nor read the Scriptures as before, but relapsed by degrees into his old ways. This continued about a month, when an attack of fever alarmed him; and he recollected how sadly he had forgotten the vows and resolutions he had formerly made in his distress and penitence. In his despair, he almost wished he had sunk in the ocean at the time when he had prayed on board the labouring ship. But he had learned something of his own frailty, and thenceforward he trusted less to good resolves, and more to

God's grace; and after this, he never relapsed into any thing like apostasy again. He now walked according to the light that was in him; and though the company of slavers certainly did not prove edifying, and he would sometimes, after a morning of earnest prayer, voluntarily spend the evening in very indifferent company, he kept from what he knew was sinful. He did not break with the world at once; he by degrees gave up first one thing, and then another, as he perceived it to be questionable and dangerous, if not sinful,—and thus he manifested his growth in grace and in the knowledge of God.

In due course, he arrived in Liverpool; and as soon as the ship's affairs were settled, he came to London, and paid another visit to Kent. More than seven years had now elapsed since his first visit, and its memorable train of consequences; but now there was no obstacle to a union with his beloved one, to whom he had remained true with an unflinching constancy during all his wanderings. Accordingly, on February 1, 1750, they were married, and lived together for more than forty years in mutual love and tenderness—the husband no less attached than the lover had been. He confesses, however, that he was more absorbed in the delights of his new state than he ought to have been, and was, to a certain extent, less religious after his marriage than before.

The young couple could not be allowed a very long time in each other's society. It was necessary that Newton should undertake another voyage; and accordingly, in August, he sailed from Liverpool as commander of a good ship in the African trade. His crew consisted of thirty persons, to whom he endeavoured to set a good example. He established service on board twice every Sunday, and treated them all with kindness and consideration. He devoted his leisure to the study of Latin. On a former voyage, he had made some progress with the language. On that occasion, his books consisted of a Delphin Horace, with an old English translation, and Castalio's Latin Bible—very indifferent helps, it must be allowed. He had no dictionary; but he was not easily daunted by difficulties; and he was able, by means of the index, to trace the words as they occurred from place to place. In this way, he made real progress—perhaps all the more solid from the very labour of the process. This voyage, he took a dictionary with him, and added Juvenal to Horace; for prose authors, he had Livy, Cæsar, and Sallust. He took especial pains with Livy, the most difficult of the three; and working very diligently during two or three voyages, he not only mastered these authors, but read, in addition, Terence, Virgil, certain writings of Cicero, and two or three modern writers, besides making some essays towards Latin composition.

He used to write constantly to his wife—keeping a kind of journal, which he sent home as opportunity occurred. His wife replied in the same way. It happened on one occasion that these letters were to be sent to St. Christopher; but, by some error, the packet was forwarded to Antigua. Knowing how punctual a correspondent Mrs. Newton was, and feeling sure that she would have written if alive, he concluded she must be dead. The anxiety was so great, that for days he could scarcely eat or sleep. After some distressing weeks of suspense, he thought of sending a small vessel to Antigua to make inquiry, and was relieved by receiving several packets of letters.

On his third voyage to Guinea, he took with him a young man who had formerly been his companion as a midshipman on board the *Harwich.* He was then a steady lad; but Newton had done his best to infect him with his own lax and sceptical principles, and with only too great success. They met again at Liverpool, and renewed their former acquaintance. Newton gave him an account of his own change of sentiment, and how it had been brought about. But his companion refused to listen, saying that Newton was the first person who had given him an idea of his liberty. That there might be time and opportunity for bringing him to a better mind, Newton took him with him on his next voyage. All was to no purpose; for he not only refused to listen, but acted as a kind of apostle of evil amongst the crew. He was also exceedingly insubordinate, so that it required all the forbearance and prudence of which Newton was master, to keep him at all in check.

At length an opportunity offered of buying a small vessel, which Newton supplied with a cargo from his own ship, gave this young man the command of it, and sent him away to trade on the ship's account. But now under no restraint, he gave the rein to his own inclinations; and the excessive irregularities of his mode of living laid him open to an attack of fever, which proved fatal. Commonly men die as they live, without remorse; but his case was an exception: conviction came, but not contrition; and he died despairing, but not repentant. On this voyage, Newton himself was in great danger from a fever; but to him the near approach of death proved a salutary influence, increasing alike the clearness of his convictions and the fervour of his faith. On his arrival at St. Christopher, he met with a man like-minded—a captain of a ship from London. For about a month, they spent every evening together on board each other's ship alternately. Newton's soul drank in what to him were the new-found delights of Christian communion. He arrived in Liverpool in August 1754, and had not intended to remain long in England; but, as he was preparing for another voyage, he was suddenly seized with an attack of apoplexy. He speedily recovered; but, not being considered in a fit state of health to proceed to Africa, he resigned his command the very day before the ship sailed. It is instructive to observe, that hitherto Newton had had little scruple about being engaged in the slave-trade. It never seems to have occurred to him that a traffic in slaves —which, to the disgrace of our country, was *then* not forbidden by its laws—was inconsistent with Christianity, and altogether contrary to its spirit. He wished, indeed, for many reasons, for a change. The protracted separations from his beloved Mary were painful; he longed to be able to enjoy the benefits of Christian worship and communion; and, though he did all in his power, even at considerable self-sacrifice, to make less odious the inhuman occupation in which he was engaged, he could not but feel an increasing repugnance to a business so conversant with bolts and shackles as his necessarily was. He had, indeed, often prayed for deliverance, and thus was the deliverance brought about. But now a fresh trial came upon him. The shock to his wife's nerves, caused by his sudden attack, proved so serious as to threaten her life. Without apparent cause, she wasted away, and medicine afforded no relief. At the same time, it was urgently necessary that Newton should find some employment; and he left home hardly expecting ever again to see her alive. But his fears on both scores were speedily relieved: he received an appointment as tide-surveyor in Liverpool, which afforded him a competency; and his wife gained strength so fast, that in two months he was able to meet her at Stone.

He now commenced the study of Greek, in order that he might read the Greek Testament, and then proceeded to learn Hebrew and Syriac. He had some idea of entering the ministry, but it was faint and distant, and hardly received a definite shape until some friends advised him to take this step, one of whom offered him a title to orders in the diocese of York. The archbishop declined to ordain him, and he modestly refrained from pushing himself forward,—preferring, as he says, to wait. In this resolve he was further strengthened by the counsel of his wife, who dissuaded him from an idea he entertained of joining one of the Nonconformist bodies.

In the year 1764, he accepted the curacy of Olney, and was ordained deacon at Buckden by Dr. Green, Bishop of Lincoln. His vicar, who had an expensive family, was non-resident, and he continued curate of Olney for nearly sixteen years. Here he became intimate with two men whose names stand out in remarkable prominence in the Christianity of that time—John Thornton, and Cowper the poet. The former made him an allowance, enabling him to fulfil adequately the duties of his ministry at Olney, which the slender stipend of a curate would hardly have allowed him to do.

In the year 1799, he was presented by Mr. Thornton to the benefice of St. Mary Woolnoth and St. Mary Woolchurch Haw, in Lombard Street, City of London. The City was at that time very different from what it has now become, and several of the bankers of Lombard Street then inhabited residences situate over their banking-premises. He was thus in the very centre of London, in an opulent neighbourhood; and the change from the country curacy of Olney to the rectory of St. Mary was great indeed. Nevertheless, there is now very little to record, save that he was known far and wide as an earnest, genial clergyman, preaching the Gospel at a time when there was still remaining a sad deadness and coldness in many churches, —though, no doubt, there was a very great improvement upon what had been witnessed in the previous half-century, when Wesley began his labours. But such a life affords little material for the biographer: its very usefulness depends on its want of exciting scenes; for, after all, the evangelisation of the world must in the main proceed, not by awakenings and startling revivals, but by the plain, earnest, persistent maintenance of religious teaching, accompanied with religious life. The gardens of the Lord are watered best by perennial springs, which make particular spots to flourish, rather than by floods of the spiritual waters,—which may, indeed, when they retire, leave a rich deposit for the future nourishment of the good seed; but, during the time of their irruption, sadly displace the ancient landmarks of the Church.

In the year 1790, after a union which had endured for forty years, he lost his wife. He was attached to her, as we know, in no ordinary degree; and during her illness, which arose from cancer, he fasted, wept, and prayed for her. Yet he preached her funeral sermon the Sunday after her death. Every one of those whose biography we have yet recorded did the like: Augustine for his mother, Bernard for his brother, Wesley for his mother, and Newton for his wife. Nor is the reason of this far to seek. It is a practical instance of the triumph of faith. Augustine understands so literally the prohibition not to sorrow as those that have no hope, that he seems to doubt whether it be not a sin even to weep. The others know and feel that thus they shall set forth the great topic which alone can comfort their own souls, and that the very effort of ministering to others will bring before themselves, in strongest relief, those consolations which can alone render their stroke bearable. The power to preach such a sermon is the sign, not of a cold heart, but of a strong will. The skilful self-analysis of Augustine shows how much pain the conflict between faith and sorrow, which raged all the while within, caused him to endure.

After his wife's death, Newton was wont to observe the anniversary of her decease as a day of seclusion. He would on this occasion compose verses to her memory. But the time was not spent in unavailing regrets. There was patience and resignation in his sorrow. He felt that, while alive, he had almost idolised her. He told a friend, after her decease, how that he would walk from London to the top of Shooter's Hill, in order to look towards the spot in which she lived: not, indeed, that it was visible from the hill, for it was far beyond,—but it gave him a satisfaction even to gaze in the direction in which she lived; and this he did, not occasionally, but always once, and sometimes twice, a week. Nor did this affection die out with the romance of courtship, but continued through their married life. Great, then, must have been the wrench when he parted from one whom he loved so dearly. But the good old man's faith was proof even against this trial. He looked upon it that God who gave had rightfully taken away, and showed himself as a practical instance of submission to His will.

His life was prolonged beyond the usual limit appointed to man. He continued preaching until he was more than eighty years of age; and though his utterance and memory began to fail at this period of his life, he was never clearer than in the pulpit. Some of his friends wished him to desist from preaching, but he declined. "I cannot stop," he said; and then, raising his voice, he added: "What! shall the old African blasphemer stop while he can speak?" But at length he could not speak: sight, hearing, and memory all failed; and his life became a blank, though easy and free from pain. But the light, though to human sight dim and flickering, still burnt on within; and what few words he could mumble out were such as became a Christian soul. The soundness of his faith, however, is not displayed by what he said upon his death-bed, but by the consistency of his godly life. He himself, and rightly, attached but little importance, as such, to death-bed utterances; so that when, in his hearing, inquiry was made as to the manner in which believers left this world, he was wont to say: "Tell me not how the man died, but how he lived." Sensible to the last, at length the feeble lamp went out, and he sank to sleep, December 21, 1807, in the eighty-second year of his age. His body lies buried in a vault of his church—a fitting resting-place. Round his tomb roars and boils the tide of London commercial life, amidst which, during his lifetime, it was his especial delight to minister.

As a writer, Newton is clear and connected; but being self-taught, and possessing but little of the learning of the schools, we cannot expect to find either deep erudition or expanded thought. He continued to be the plain, honest sailor, who, having been fully convinced of the truth himself, laboured diligently and uninterruptedly to convince others. Good sense, a kind heart, and earnest piety, make up a character which commands both love and respect. And though he has no claim to be ranked in the same category of usefulness as an Augustine or a Bernard, and has nothing of the organising power of a Wesley, or the eloquence of a Whitefield, his wonderful conversion and earnest life entitle him to a subordinate place in a group which includes these great names as its principal figures.

CHARLES SIMEON: THE DESPISED EXALTED.

Faith patient in Well-doing.

"I intend neither to deny, dissemble, defend, nor excuse any of his faults. 'We have this treasure,' says the Apostle, 'in earthen vessels;' and he that shall endeavour to prove a pitcher of clay to be a pot of gold, will take great pains to small purpose."—FULLER.

LIFE OF CHARLES SIMEON:

THE DESPISED EXALTED.

HARLES SIMEON was the fourth and youngest son of Richard Simeon and Elizabeth Hutton. His parents were of good family, being descended from the Simeons of Pyrton, in Oxfordshire. His brothers were Richard, who died young; John, senior Master in Chancery, and in 1815 created a baronet; and Edward, a merchant of London, and bank-director, who amassed a large fortune. Charles, the youngest, was born at Reading, September 24, 1759. Of his early history little is known; he was educated at Eton, and was in due course admitted on the foundation, and, when nineteen years of age, succeeded to a scholarship at King's College, Cambridge. As a schoolboy, he was remarkable for his energy and vigour. Horsemanship was his favourite exercise,—few persons being better judges than he was of the points of a good horse, or more skilful in the management of one. In feats of activity and strength, he was preëminent. His old friend, Dr. Goodall, writes to him: "I doubt if you could now snuff a candle with your feet, or jump over half a dozen chairs in succession;" and then, in Latin, follow these words: "But why do I remind you of these things? at seventy-three, we are admonished that we have something better to think of."

He was not, however, a great favourite with his school-fellows; for, as a boy especially, he exhibited some peculiarities of temper which provoked their ridicule. He was vain, impetuous, and self-conscious; and these were faults which dimmed, to a certain extent, his real excellences. In after life, also, the imperfections of his character are to be found in the display of these same faults, or rather foibles; but perhaps in this very circumstance is to be discerned the power of that Spirit which dwelt within him. Few men lived more consistent Christian lives than he did, or more completely overcame defects of character, which, nevertheless, remained apparent to the very end of his life. He was irascible, also, and would, in the heat of passion, say things which, in cooler moments, he would retract; and, as too often happens, these outbursts of temper were occasioned by the veriest trifles. But in this is manifest the power of his religious experience, that, as his character matured, he became less subject to this fault, and more and more displayed his kind and forgiving temper. It might have been expected that such a man would have been sometimes excited to revenge,—and Simeon often received very great provocation; but if he spoke unadvisedly, he rarely or never acted unkindly.

He has left behind him an autobiography, in which he speaks of his early life in language of strong reprobation: "My vanity, my folly, my wickedness," he says, "God alone knoweth, or can bear to know." But it does not appear, however just his judgment of himself may be from the point of view which a Christian will adopt in self-examination, that, judged of by the standard a biographer must take, it can be admitted without qualification. He was regarded by his masters and school-fellows as steady and earnest; and though, no doubt, not always rising superior to the temptations with which his boyish life was surrounded, his general conduct was such as to merit the esteem of his companions.

His first rising convictions began at school. About two years before he left, one of the fast-days on account of the American war was appointed to be observed. He was particularly struck with the idea of a whole nation uniting in fasting and prayer, and regarded himself as one who more especially needed humiliation, on account of his own sins. Accordingly, he spent the day with unusual strictness; shutting himself up within his study, and contenting himself, in the matter of food, with a single hard-boiled egg. "From this time," says a school-fellow, "his dress and manners became more plain and unfashionable; he also kept a small box, fitted with different compartments, into one or other of which, when he had said or done any thing he considered wrong, he would put money for the poor." The existence of this box became known to his school-fellows, who made a song about him, ridiculing his strictness and devotion, the chorus of which contained an allusion to this box. The ridicule so far prevailed upon him, that he gave up something of his strictness—he speaks in his autobiography as if entirely; but this was hardly so. The good seed was about to spring up and grow, and bear fruit to perfection.

On his arrival at King's College, he was informed that he would be expected in about three weeks' time to attend the holy communion. He considered himself sadly unfit for so sacred an ordinance, but at once set himself to prepare. He bought *The Whole Duty of Man*,—the only religious book of the kind he knew of,—and spent the three weeks in preparation so earnest, that he made himself quite ill with reading and fasting and prayer. His first communion was received in fear and trembling, under a deep sense of his own unworthiness; but it was a blessed one, nevertheless. From that day forward, he never relapsed; and, before the Easter communion, he knew something of the blessedness of a heart at peace with God.

The service in his college-chapel was a great

source of comfort to him. At that time there was much to be desired in the way of reverent performance in this, as in other college-chapels in Cambridge; and that most noble and magnificent building—which none can behold without a feeling of awe—was profaned by the carelessness of those who were unworthy of the sanctuary in which they ministered: but a devout heart can find spiritual food in circumstances where others are only coldness and deadness. Matters at King's College are now, and have been for many years, in a very different state in this respect; and the writer, remembering the many hours of devotion spent in this chapel when his own was closed in vacation-time, can fully indorse the sentiment of this man of God, that, if we do not enjoy the Liturgy, it is not from defects in it, but from our own want of earnestness,—for "no prayers in the world could be better suited to our wants, or more delightful to our souls."

There was displayed in him that same desire to benefit others which is so marked a characteristic of earnest religious impressions. Those not conversant with the habits of the University of Cambridge, need to be told that the students are there waited on by elderly female servants, known as "bed-makers." A very stringent code of etiquette, which no student can venture to neglect, regulates the relation between bed-maker and undergraduate, and is found effectually to prevent any of the possible evils which might otherwise arise. Simeon's zeal and earnestness was able to overcome a difficulty which must have been very great to one so sensitive. He formed a Bible-class among the bed-makers of the college. He says: "I adopted a measure which must have appeared most singular to others, and which perhaps a more matured judgment might have disapproved; but I acted in the simplicity of my heart, and I am persuaded God accepted it at my hands. I told my servant that, as she and the other servants were prevented almost entirely from going to church, I would do my best to instruct them on a Sunday evening, if they chose to come to me for that purpose. Several of them thankfully availed themselves of the offer, and came to me." His labours seem to have been productive of little benefit to his hearers, but these opportunities were not lost upon himself.

In the long vacation,—which at Cambridge extends from June to October,—he went home. He was greatly desirous of introducing family prayers; but, fearing that neither his father nor brother would assent if he applied directly to them, he assembled the servants for worship in his own room, leaving it to his brother to join him or not, as he pleased. To his great joy, his brother cordially seconded his efforts, and his father made no objection: and thus this good and pious custom was introduced into the household.

On Trinity Sunday, the 26th of May 1782, he was ordained. Being now a fellow of his college, he needed no special cure; the college-title, as it is called, being always deemed sufficient. He was anxious, however, to work to the utmost, and he served in the church of St. Edward, in the town of Cambridge, as curate. He had attended regularly at St. Edward's for some time, and, being the only gownsman there, expected that Mr. Atkinson, the incumbent, would take some notice of him; but he waited for a considerable time before the desired opportunity occurred,—indeed, he had now been in Cambridge three years, and had never found a single friend like-minded. At length Mr. Atkinson asked him to come and drink tea with him, inviting also a friend to meet him. The conversation did not at that time take a serious turn, but the introduction enabled Simeon to ask Mr. Atkinson in return; and it so happened, from the unexpected absence of a guest, that they were alone together. Simeon took the opportunity to give expression to his thoughts—speaking of himself as a sinner. Mr. Atkinson was struck by this. He had noticed the singular undergraduate of King's, and set him down as a pharisee; but he now at once opened his heart to him; and the next day he introduced him to John Venn, who became a most intimate friend. John Venn introduced Simeon to his father; and in this pious and aged clergyman he found one to whom he could look up for instruction and advice, and who had great influence on his after life.

It appears that, during the early part of his career,

Simeon lived a strangely isolated life. The writer entered the university only four years after his death, and was at once introduced to those on whom his mantle may be said to have descended. Several traditions were then current as to what he had been in his undergraduate days. It was said that at one time he was so completely cut by his acquaintance, in consequence of his religious views, that he had not a single friend even in Cambridge, the place of all others where men form friendships which often last through life. He was obliged, therefore, to take solitary walks; and it is related that, meeting a gownsman who spoke to him in a friendly way, he burst into tears at a circumstance so unusual, this being the first act of kindness he had received for months. This may be an exaggerated statement, and worth no more than such stories commonly are; but its currency at that time is significant. His name, also, was contracted into a term of reproach; and the writer remembers that "Sim" still lingered in the university as a designation of those more than usually serious and punctual in attendance on chapel and other religious duties. On one occasion, when the degrees were being conferred in the Senate-House, and when, as is well known to Cambridge men, the undergraduates attending in the gallery are wont to express themselves somewhat freely and pointedly on men and things, a voice from this gallery proposed "Three groans for the Sims." "What is a Sim?" shouted another voice in reply.

"Qui simulat"—"He who simulates"—was the answer; and this ready repartee saved the poor Sims from the groans called for, in the laughter which arose.

Having now become acquainted with Mr. Atkinson, he undertook the care of his church during the long vacation. In the space of a month or six weeks, the church became quite crowded,—a fact the more to be noticed, as Cambridge is comparatively empty in the long vacation. On the very first day of his ministrations at St. Edward's, a remarkable occurrence took place. In returning from church, he was arrested by the loud wrangling of a man and his wife, who lived in a narrow thoroughfare called St. Edward's Passage. The door being open, he entered the house, and expostulated with them on the sin of absenting themselves unnecessarily from the Lord's house, and disturbing by their unseemly conduct those who had been there. He then knelt down to pray for them; and persons passing by, attracted by the novelty of the scene, gradually collected, until the room was full.

His own family were, however, offended at his zeal, and remonstrated with him; but his convictions were too deep to be thus shaken; and in a while they all became such as he himself was, won over by his goodness. His eldest brother was taken ill, and Charles hastened to him. The others would have kept him away at that time, fearing lest he should disturb his mind; but Richard was comforted and edified by his brother's ministrations, and departed in peace. His father was inconsolable during the progress of the last illness; but, after his son's death, he too found comfort and resignation. It seemed desirable that Charles should now reside with his father, and every thing was arranged, so that he was on the point of leaving Cambridge. But just at that time the incumbent of Trinity Church, Cambridge, died. He asked his father to make application to the Bishop of Ely, the patron, for the presentation,—which he did. The parishioners wished for the appointment of a Mr. Hammond, who had been curate, whom they immediately appointed lecturer, and petitioned the bishop in his favour. The living, without the lectureship, was not worth more than 50*l.* per annum. The bishop, considering that the parishioners had not done right in filling up the lectureship before they petitioned him, refused to present Mr. Hammond under any circumstances, and Simeon was appointed. But the parish were so angry, that for years he could make but little way with them. No doubt, also, there was some fault on the other side. His manner was peculiar,—and, in those days, displays of fervour in the pulpit were not usual; but the faults were superficial, the religion was deep.

In the year 1786, he preached before the university for the first time. His friends came, afraid lest he should say something that would give offence; his enemies, and there were many, were on the watch, to find occasion against him. The gallery was crowded with undergraduates, some of whom came, it is said, to *scrape*—an unseemly interruption of the preacher, by movements, apparently accidental, of the feet upon the floor—at that period not unusual, but now altogether a thing of the past. But, after a few opening sentences, all were riveted by the earnestness of the preacher and the clearness of his expression. Of two young men who had come as scoffers, one was heard to say to the other: "Well, Simeon is no fool, however." "Fool!" replied his companion; "did you ever hear such a sermon before?" This continued opposition, however, was of great service to him—he could even rejoice in it, as teaching him that humility and self-abnegation which he was conscious he so much needed. He had, indeed, a good deal to bear beside the opposition from his parishioners before spoken of,—the undergraduates would often create a disturbance in his church. Simeon had introduced an evening service; and this, though now so common, was then regarded as a novelty, and supposed to savour of Methodism. It was principally at this service that the interruption took place. He used accordingly, immediately on the conclusion of the service, to go to the great north door, and apprehend any gownsman who should insult, as they sometimes did, members of the congregation as they left the church. He would entreat those who were inclined to resist not to make him ask their names. If they still proved obstinate, he would direct them to call on him the next morning,—

and no instance occurred of refusal. On one occasion, an undergraduate broke a window, and then immediately after entered the church. This was an outrage not to be suffered, and Simeon appealed to the vice-chancellor of the university, who offered to proceed with the culprit in any way that Simeon should desire. To have sent him away from the university—the usual punishment for a very serious offence—would have been to blight all his prospects. Simeon therefore insisted that the young man should read a written apology publicly to the congregation for his bad conduct; and as, naturally, he did not read it very distinctly, Simeon afterwards read it out himself. This well-timed act of severity proved sufficiently deterrent, and the congregation were not again annoyed.

The record of Simeon's life is indeed a remarkable illustration of our motto: it was an instance of what might be accomplished by patient continuance in well-doing. Gradually, but unceasingly, did he win his way to the end of a long life, until at length few men were more respected and honoured than he. Yet the road was an uphill one; and for years he met with the most strenuous opposition from those who were of a different school from himself. The truth was, that a reform was much needed at that time within the Church. Those who were called High Churchmen then were very different indeed from those who bear that name now; and, if opposed to the Evangelicals of that time, they would certainly have had little more sympathy with those whom we now call High Churchmen. They were High Church, in a theoretical attachment to the formularies of the Church; but did very little indeed to carry out her principles into practice. The services in the churches—at least, in country churches—were, with some happy exceptions, performed in a very slovenly manner. The vestments of the Church were a surplice,—too often not over-clean, —with hood, but without stole, and the academical gown at the sermon. The hymnal was Brady and Tate, sung to the monotonous notes of a grind-organ, or the more elaborate, but hardly less artistic, performance of a village-choir. If an anthem was attempted, "Vital Spark" was regarded as the highest expression both of musical art and spiritual devotion. The rubric before the Communion Service, which directs that it be administered three times a year at least, was read as though to be understood not much more often than three times. Such architectural deformities as whitewash, sash-windows, and high deal pews, reigned every where supreme. The writer, indeed, recollects being taken, as a child, to what was then a fashionable church, in a fashionable watering-place: the ecclesiastical arrangements were such as would, no doubt, be pronounced decidedly "low," by an Anglican of the present day; but the spectacle of two clergymen, in clean surplices, scarfs, and hoods, kneeling at a communion-table, covered with a bright crimson communion-cloth, with the accessories of carpet, kneeling-stools, and morocco-bound service-books, was to him an unwonted display of ritual magnificence. At the church in which he was accustomed to attend, the Communion Service was invariably read from the desk, it being alleged that the chancel was so blocked up with pews and galleries, that the service would have been inaudible if read at its proper place. The worship was of a piece with its accessories. The prayers were read in a perfunctory and slovenly way; the sermons were written compositions, without life or unction; and if sometimes possessing the merit of being short, they were always afflicted with the defect of being tedious.

It was Simeon and his followers who were the leaders of a reform in these matters; and they began with the sermons. This was but natural. Simeon's power was that of a preacher; and his peculiar excellence was a lucid arrangement of his matter, joined with an earnest statement of evangelical truth. He enjoyed special facilities for making his influence felt. His ministry was attended by those destined to orders. He for years, with increasing popularity and usefulness, held meetings amongst the undergraduates, with the express object of preparation for the ministry. There was, as he advanced in life, an energy and sincerity of manner, which gave him a more than fatherly authority over the young men who came up from year to year. He was perpetually engaged in finding suitable curacies for those who were desirous of entering the ministry. He watched over those newly ordained, and gave them most valuable suggestions as to voice, manner, and disposal of time. He urged all to pursue diligently the studies of the university; and thus many of those he sent forth went to their work with all the advantages which high academical distinction conferred. No wonder, then, that he won his way. Yet it was uphill work. The prejudice against him and his ministry was very strong, as the following circumstance, known to the writer, will testify. A young man applied to a clergyman in the metropolis for his curacy, with a title to orders. His abilities were even then known to be considerable; and he afterwards took a high position both as a preacher and parochial clergyman. His testimonials were of the highest character; and all other arrangements being satisfactorily concluded, a personal interview was asked, and intending incumbent and curate were mutually pleased with each other. The latter was about to leave the room, when the former said, "I had forgotten to ask one question: What church did you attend at Cambridge?" "Trinity," was the reply. "Then, sir, I regret to say that I must consider our negotiation at an end." But this opposition died slowly away; and, not many years after this circumstance occurred, there were few men who would not have listened with respect to a recommendation of Mr. Simeon's.

His personal kindness was great; and many were indebted to him for help towards their studies. Amongst others, Henry Kirke White, the poet, whose biography will be touched upon subsequently, was enabled to enter the university, and largely experienced, during his short course, the *fatherly* care, as he terms it, of Simeon, who watched the rising talent and earnest piety of the young genius. David Brown, Henry Martyn, John Sergeant, Thomas Thomason, Bishop Corrie, and others still living, of equal repute with these, were happy to call themselves disciples of this good man.

Simeon was a great promoter, and in part founder, of the Church Missionary Society, the Bible Society, and the Society for promoting Christianity among the Jews. In this last he always took especial interest, and was for many years its main stay. The peculiar principles of all these societies are well known, as they have now been long before the world; and that they have done good service in the cause of Christ's Gospel, no earnest Christian, whatever be his views, can doubt. Simeon was always an attached member of the Church to which he belonged. It is quite true that he gave some offence to the High Churchmen of his day by preaching, when north of the Tweed, in some of the Presbyterian sanctuaries, alleging that, as the king attended service in Presbyterian churches, the clergyman might do so too. But it is a curious incident in the history of religious party, and one which deserves careful consideration, that there were high Presbyterians as well as high Episcopalians; and these had sufficient influence to obtain the enactment of a rule, by which Anglican clergymen are restrained from preaching in Presbyterian pulpits. The rule, indeed, was general; but it was felt that it was aimed principally at Simeon. The irregularities, however, of which he was guilty, were not only slight and excusable in themselves, but were confined to the earlier years of his ministry. As an earnest man and an honest man, he of course did all he could to forward his own views; and thus he became the leader of the modern Evangelical school of the Church of England. How well that school did its work is evident in the state of things we now behold,—multiplied services, earnest congregations every where. And if the followers of this good man—going, as followers are wont to do, beyond the teachings of their master—have seemed to underrate the value of the apostolical order of their Church, then that High-Church revival we are now witnessing will supply this lack,—and the time will come, though not yet, when it too will be contemplated from a distance sufficiently great to behold its real proportions. It will then be seen that the Lord of the Church ever accepts what is really good and scriptural in every Church movement, and purges out the errors of those who take part in it, that thus they may bring forth more fruit.

As Simeon rose into eminence, so does his life

follow the law of biographies, and become less and less eventful; but, in its way, it was, perhaps, one of the most successful ever recorded. "Contrast," writes Bishop Wilson of Calcutta, "the commencement and close of his course. He stood for many years alone; he was long opposed, ridiculed, shunned; his doctrines were misrepresented, his little peculiarities of voice and manner were satirised, disturbances were raised in his church; he was a person not taken into account, nor considered in the light of a regular clergyman in the Church. Sad was the beginning of things: but mark the close. For the last portion of his ministry, all was rapidly changing. He was invited repeatedly to take courses of sermons before the university. The same great principles that he preached were avowed from almost every pulpit in Cambridge. His church was crowded with students. . . . In 1835, the university went up to present an address to the king. The vice-chancellor wished him to attend; and when the members of the Senate were assembled, he made public inquiry whether he was present, that he might be presented to his majesty, and publicly expressed his regret that illness had prevented him from attending."

His aim, however, was as steady as his principles; he from the first determined to sacrifice every thing for the work's sake. He never married. His labours were absolutely without emolument for half a century. He refused all the livings in the gift of his college, which came to him in right of his fellowship,—some of them involving positions which almost any other man would have taken as a matter of course. He persuaded his elder brother not to leave him his fortune, because, had he done so, he would have been compelled to vacate his fellowship, and with it his post of usefulness in the university. He devoted all the large property which he inherited, or made by the sale of his writings, to the work in which he was engaged, content to discharge the simple, unostentatious duties of a fellow resident in the university: the greatest change in his life being, apparently, removal to another set of rooms in his college, a little more convenient for his classes, and commanding a little more quiet for private devotion.

In this most useful life, he survived to the age of seventy-eight. He remained hale and strong almost to the last; and though, as eternity drew into sight, he thought more and more seriously on the great change, there was no sensible diminution of animation and energy in his sermons and lectures. On Thursday evening, September 15, he preached as usual, and again on Sunday; on Tuesday, he was in high health and spirits, and talked of the journey he proposed to take the next day to Ely with great delight. But even now there was a presentiment upon him that his time was near at hand. He had been appointed select preacher for the November following, and he spoke as if he knew that the labour of this duty would in some measure exhaust his strength. Dr. Allen had just been appointed Bishop of Ely, and Simeon was anxious to pay his respects to his new diocesan. The day fixed for this visit—Wednesday, September 21—was damp and chilly; and Simeon, trusting to his health and vigour, was more thinly clad than usual. The bishop received him with marked kindness and attention, and proposed that they should go over the cathedral together. They lingered too long, and Simeon took a chill, which displayed itself the following day in a violent attack of rheumatism. He was unable to preach as usual in the evening, for which service he had prepared a discourse on the words, "Lord, teach us to pray" (Luke xi. 1). This was the last subject he ever prepared for the pulpit.

Saturday, September 24, was his birthday; he had entered his seventy-eighth year. He rose early, and, though still very feeble, was better, and by degrees so far recovered, that hopes were entertained that he was convalescent. But a relapse came on about the middle of October, and he was again confined to his bed; and on Friday, October 21, all hope of recovery was taken away. But he could still lay firm hold of the hope which was in him. He said, as his friends spoke of the prospect before him, "I have not a doubt or fear. I cannot have more peace." A large number of persons were in the room, and he said nothing more at that time; but when they were gone, he spoke to the friend whom he took chiefly into his confidence, and expressed his desire that he might, when his last moments arrived, be left alone. He was the more urgent, as it appeared to him that his friends had come into the room expecting his immediate dissolution. He said: "I wish to be alone with my God, and to lie before Him as a poor, wretched, hell-deserving sinner,—yes, as a poor, hell-deserving sinner; but I would also look to Him as my all-forgiving God, as my all-sufficient God, as my all-atoning God, as my covenant-keeping God. There I would lie before Him, as the vilest of the vile, and the lowest of the low, and the poorest of the poor. Now, this is what I have to say,—I wish to be alone; don't let people come round, to get up a scene."

But the end was not just yet. On the following day he rallied, and began to make preparations for the November sermons. On the Wednesday following, he was worse again; and this time he felt that the messenger had come which was really to call him to his rest. "The decree has," he said, "gone forth; from this hour, I am a dying man. Death is far sweeter than life, under such circumstances. I will wait patiently for my dismission." His time was spent in meditation on Scripture, especially during the sleepless hours of night. At this time, also, occurred the anniversary sermon for the Jews, and he dictated a short address, to be read to the undergraduates at their meeting, consisting principally of Scripture: Ezek. xxxvi. 22-24, Jer. xxxii. 41, Zeph. iii. 17,

Rom. xi. 28; and this was the last public act of his life.

He was naturally anxious about his flock at Trinity, which he had tended for so many years, and accordingly he wrote to the bishop, asking for the presentation for one who, he believed, would carry on his own good work. The bishop assented in the very kindest manner, intimating, at the same time, that, had no such request been made, it had been his intention to make the appointment Simeon suggested.

There was a rapid maturing of his character from the beginning of his illness, and a corresponding diminution of that haste and irritability which had often led him into unadvised, and perhaps unchristian, temper. Amongst other instances, the following is characteristic. A fellow of his own college, who had often grieved him by acts of discourtesy, was lying upon his death-bed, suffering acutely, and altogether in a state so wretched and distressing as to deter his friends from visiting him. Simeon sent to inquire after him every day, with some kind expression of sympathy. He could not forbear observing, "Well, Simeon does not forget me, but sends daily to inquire after me, ill as *he* is."

During the last few days, he suffered greatly; but these pains of death did not cause him to fall from his hope. "Do you," he asked of his friends, "see any sting of death here? No, it is all taken away. Does not this prove that my principles are not founded on fancies or enthusiasm, but that there is a reality in them?—and I find them sufficient to support me in death."

On Friday, November 11, several sympathising friends stood beside him, lamenting his protracted sufferings. He was unable to speak; but being lifted up from his bed, he clasped his hands together, in the attitude of devout prayer; he then stretched them towards his friends, and thus took his final leave. The following day, he still lived, but was unconscious; and at two o'clock on Sunday, when the great bell at St. Mary's was tolling for the university sermon, with a faint struggle, the spirit departed.

HENRY KIRKE WHITE.

Faith not striving lawfully.

"Read ye that run the awful truth
With which I charge my page,—
A worm is in the bud of youth,
And at the root of age."

"'Tis the only discipline we are born for;
All studies else are but as circular lines,
And death the centre where they must all meet."

COWPER *and* MASSINGER,
quoted by Southey.

LIFE OF HENRY KIRKE WHITE.

WE have already been introduced to the undergraduate of St. John's College who, by the kindness of Simeon, is able to pursue his studies at the university. We propose now to give some details of his life. He serves as an example of those who attend to the injunction, "Whatsoever thy hand findeth to do, do it with all thy might;" but he forgot that other aphorism, "Be not over-wise," and so destroyed himself.

Henry Kirke White was born in Nottingham, March 21, 1785. His father was John White, a butcher in that town; and his mother, whose maiden name was Mary Neville, was of a respectable Staffordshire family. At three years of age, he went to a school kept by a Mrs. Garrington. Young as he was, his good, kind-hearted schoolmistress perceived that she had no common child to instruct, and prophesied his future eminence. He thus describes his school-experience :

> "Much did I grieve on that ill-fated morn,
> When I was first to school reluctant borne.
> Severe I thought the dame, though oft she tried
> To soothe my swelling spirits when I sighed;
> And oft, when harshly she reproved, I wept,
> To my lone corner broken-hearted crept,
> And thought of tender home, where anger never kept.
> But soon inured to alphabetic toils,
> Alert I met the dame with jocund smiles;
> First at my form, my task for ever true,
> A little favourite rapidly I grew;
> And oft she stroked my head with fond delight,
> Held me a pattern to the dunce's sight,
> And, as she gave my diligence its praise,
> Talked of the honours of my future days."

These lines were written, probably, when he was about fifteen, and certainly justified the complacent prophecies of his schoolmistress. To her, indeed, in the same poem, he ascribes his leaning towards poetry. She would tell her pupils stories

> "of innocence foredoomed to bleed,
> Of wicked guardians bent on bloody deed,
> Of little children murdered as they slept;
> While at each pause we wrung our hands and wept.
> * * * * * *
> Beloved moment! then 'twas first I caught
> The first foundation of romantic thought,
> Then first I shed bold fancy's thrilling tear,
> Then first that poesy charmed mine infant ear."

When about six, he was removed to the school

of the Rev. John Blanchard, the best in Nottingham. Here he learned writing, arithmetic, and French. At seven years of age, he wrote a tale of a Swiss emigrant, which he gave to the servant. This girl was his pupil; he would quietly creep into the kitchen, and teach her to read and write. When he was about eleven, he wrote a separate theme for every boy in his class, which consisted of about twelve or fourteen. The quality was so superior to that usually produced by the boys, that the master expressed surprise, saying he had never known them write so well on any subject before. His genius, however, was but little appreciated at school; and one of the ushers informed his mother that he was incorrigible, and that his teachers could do nothing with him. In consequence of some differences between Mr. Blanchard and his father, he was removed; and, had it not been that his next instructor judged more favourably of him, he would probably have become, what his father at that time wished to make him, a butcher in Nottingham.

Henry had, during his school-time, to attend to his father's business; and one whole day in each week was spent in carrying the butcher's tray; but his nature revolted from such a calling; and, as an alternative, he was, at the age of fourteen, placed in a stocking-loom. But he wanted some employment which would occupy his brain. His father was averse to this; but his mother listened sympathisingly to his complaints, and at length procured him the situation of clerk in the office of Messrs. Coldham and Enfield, solicitors and town-clerks of Nottingham. Here he was to serve two years before he was articled.

He was now advised to study the Latin language. His employers were in very large practice; and he conscientiously allowed nothing to come between him and his duty to them. Nevertheless, with the very little leisure at his command, he contrived, in ten months, to make such progress as to read Horace with tolerable facility. He also began Greek; and, to save time, would exercise himself in declining Greek nouns and verbs as he went to and from the office; and thus, in hours which others would have considered waste, he mastered this most difficult part of the language. From this time he contracted the habit of employing his mind in study during his walks, which he continued to the end of his life.

His whole leisure was now devoted to intellectual improvement. He had a little room given him, which was called his study; and here he took his meals. His mother began to be alarmed: she feared that such severe and unremitting application would destroy his health; but he refused to listen. He certainly made wonderful progress. The greater part of his time was given to the duties of his profession,—in which he speedily became so well qualified, as to be most useful in his office, both in the knowledge and in the practice of the law. In addition, he studied Greek and Latin. He was a good Italian scholar, and had acquired some knowledge of Spanish and Portuguese. He had a respectable acquaintance with chemistry and general physics. He had given some little practice to drawing, and could play the piano by ear; but the fine arts were made secondary, lest they should interfere with more important objects.

There was a literary society in Nottingham at this time, to which, soon after leaving school, he endeavoured to obtain admission; but he was rejected, on the ground of youth. After repeated attempts and repeated failures, he was elected a member, through the interest of his friends. Soon after his election, he proposed to give the society a lecture. This proposal was acceded to; but the society met far more to gratify curiosity than in any expectation of an intellectual feast. He lectured upon *Genius* for over two hours, speaking extempore. His audience were so charmed with his discourse, that he received the unanimous thanks of the society; and soon after, he was elected professor of literature.

His diligence and earnestness in the profession of the law remained unabated; but now he began to have higher aspirations, and to cast his eyes with longing toward the universities. He had begun at an early age to try his hand at literature. A periodical called the *Juvenile Library* offered from time to time prizes for boys' essays on various subjects. Henry used to enter the lists; and he obtained a prize of a silver medal for a translation from Horace at the age of fifteen; and, the year after, a pair of twelve-inch globes, for an imaginary tour from London to Edinburgh. He then became a correspondent of the *Monthly Mirror;* and this introduced him to Mr. Capel Lofft, and the proprietor, Mr. Hill. They encouraged him, about the close of the year 1802, to prepare a little volume of poems for the press,—hoping that this publication, either by the success of its sale, or the notice it might excite, would enable him to prosecute his studies at college, and so fit himself for orders.

It was considered desirable that he should obtain a patroness for his book, to whom it should be dedicated. This would give him a certain *prestige*, in Nottingham especially, which would doubtless be of service to him in the object which he had in view. The Countess of Derby was first applied to; but she courteously and kindly declined,—sending, however, two guineas, as a subscription to the work. The Duchess of Devonshire was next solicited to act as patroness to the young poet; and the manuscript was left at Devonshire House, with a letter. No notice was taken of it for some time; and poor Henry began to fear lest he should not only fail in his request, but lose his manuscript as well. His brother Neville then went to Devonshire House, in hopes, if not of obtaining an interview, at least of recovering the papers. He called several times, but in vain; and at length, after waiting four hours, was able to get back from the servants the precious manuscript, having tired out their insolence by his own importunity. The brothers had now given up all thoughts of a dedication, when they were urged to make one more trial. They obtained a letter of introduction to the Duchess, who granted an interview, and gave consent to the volume being dedicated to her. In due course, the poems were printed; and the Duchess received the usual presentation-copy, bound in morocco,—of which no notice was ever taken.

The poems were sent to all the existing reviews, with a letter stating the object with which the poems were printed. The *Monthly Review* took notice of the poems, indeed; but only to condemn. Henry felt this bitterly, and wrote to remonstrate. But the criticism was not so disastrous as he expected it to be; on the contrary, it incidentally proved a great benefit,—for the review called forth no less a champion than Robert Southey; who, seeing the real merit of the poems, and commiserating with the young author, wrote to offer his assistance, and afterwards became his biographer, and the editor of his posthumous works, —moved to this "by the indignation which he felt at perusing a criticism at once so cruel and so stupid."

The poems fell into the hands of several influential friends, who endeavoured to forward his views; and interest was made for him at Cambridge, in order to obtain the necessary funds to enable him to enter the university. Hopes were held out to him of success, and his employers gave him a month's leave of absence, for the benefit of uninterrupted study and change of air. He took a small lodging in the village of Wilford, near Clifton Woods, on the banks of the Trent,—a place which he had already immortalised in his poem of "Clifton Grove." But at the end of the month intelligence reached him that the efforts made in his behalf had entirely failed. The disappointment was great. He considered that he had lost valuable time in his profession, and set himself with greater zeal than ever to redeem the time thus wasted. He now allowed himself no relaxation, and scarcely any sleep. He would read till one, two, or three in the morning, and then rise again at five. His mother used every effort to dissuade him from exertions which had now passed all bounds of prudence, but in vain. He would not listen; and his disobedience in this respect was not long in bringing its own punishment. Yet, bitter as his disappointment was, he knew how to use it aright. He touchingly sings the tale of his own sorrow:

"Come, Disappointment, come;
Though from Hope's summit hurled,
Still, rigid nurse, thou art forgiven;
For thou, severe, wert sent from heaven,
To wean me from the world—
To turn mine eye
From vanity,
And point to scenes of bliss which never die.

Come, Disappointment, come;
  Thou art not stern to me;
Sad monitress, I own thy sway;
A votary sad, in early day,
  I bend my knee to thee.
      From sun to sun,
      My race will run:
  I only bow, and say, my God, Thy will be done."

He had learned by this time where to go for consolation; although, like many others, his practice was behind his principles.

Yet a great change had already come over Henry's religious views and feelings. He had adopted deistical opinions, and was careless about all religion. He had a friend of the name of Almond, who afterwards became rector of St. Peter's, Nottingham. It so happened that Mr. Almond, being accidentally present at a death-bed, was so struck with what he there saw of the power and influence of the Gospel, that he determined for the future to renounce all pursuits and friendships which would not conduce to his spiritual improvement. Amongst his friends, the one he dreaded most to meet was Henry Kirke White, being particularly afraid of his raillery. He anxiously shunned his company, until Henry—who would not suffer an intimacy to be broken off, he knew not why—called upon him, and asked him for what cause he now avoided himself and others of his acquaintance with whom he had hitherto been intimate. Mr. Almond, who was reluctantly persuaded to see him, told him that his religious views were now altogether changed, and intimated that he was a believer in revelation, and that he was prepared to defend his opinions and conduct, if Henry would allow the Bible to be the word of truth and standard of appeal. Henry answered, "Good God! you surely regard me in a worse light than I deserve." His friend then pointed out that he had said this because, having heard him use some disparaging expression concerning the Scriptures, he imagined they could have no common ground; and then proceeded further to unfold his views. Henry, evidently ill at ease, was impressed. His friend, instead of being assailed in a tone of triumphant superiority, as he expected to be, found Henry disposed to listen patiently to him; and they parted for that time, his friend putting into his hands Scott's *Force of Truth.* This work produced little effect; but conscience accomplished what argument failed to do. He felt that there was no rest or happiness apart from the Gospel; and the conviction gathered strength from day to day. When Mr. Almond was about to enter the University of Cambridge, on the evening before his departure, Henry requested that he would come up with him into his little study. As soon as they were alone, he burst into tears, and declared that his anguish of mind was insupportable. He entreated his friend to kneel down and pray for him. They prayed heartily together, mingling their tears and supplications. When his friend took leave, Henry exclaimed, "What must I do? You are the only friend to whom I can apply in this agonising state, and you are about to leave me. My literary associates are all inclined to Deism, and I have no one with whom I can communicate."

When Mr. Almond arrived in Cambridge, he endeavoured to interest some persons in Henry's behalf, who might be able to help him in what was the great object of his life,—that of passing through the university, and taking holy orders. At first, he was not very successful; but Dr. Dealtry, the then mathematical lecturer of Trinity College, and Henry Martyn, who was at that time fellow of St. John's, interested themselves in his favour. Martyn was but a few years his senior, earnest and ardent, and took great interest in him; he entered his name on his own college,—a college which has had the honour of being preëminent in its efforts to assist poor men of genius. Just at this time there seemed to be a little difficulty, but it was removed. White came up with an introduction to Mr. Simeon. At first, Mr. Simeon was averse to see him; but an interview dispelled all difficulty; and by his generosity, and that of an unknown friend, the means were supplied to enable him to enter at college.

White was a sizar of St. John's College. In ancient times, the sizars at Cambridge, like the servitors at Oxford, performed menial duties; but this has long become obsolete,—and a sizar now experiences no other disadvantages than those which necessarily attach to limited means; and if he be known to be a man likely to take a high place in any of the examinations of the university, the open declaration of poverty, which the acceptance of a sizarship implies, enables him to avoid many expenses, without in any corresponding degree diminishing his social status. Kirke White was, therefore, now in the most favourable position possible for accomplishing the end in view, and he at once began to work with his accustomed assiduity. Soon after he entered, a university scholarship was to be competed for. To obtain a university scholarship is considered a higher honour than the attainment of a college scholarship, because the competition, in such a case, is amongst the picked men of the whole university. He was advised, by those who knew his powers, to sit for this scholarship, and accordingly he set to work with such over-diligence, that, when the time came, his strength failed, and he was unable to go in to the examination. But this was not the only disadvantage: his college examination was impending, and he had given his attention to the scholarship subjects; and a failure at the annual college examination would have had a very disastrous effect upon his future prospects. He had but a fortnight to prepare what other men had been about for several months. Again he read beyond his strength, and at the time of examination went, with tears in his eyes, to his tutor, Mr. Catton, to tell him that he could not go into the hall to be examined. Mr. Catton advised him to hold on during the six days of examination, and by the help of strong medicines he did so, and came out first; but the effort was made at the expense of his life. His health was now completely broken. Possibly, had he rested entirely during the long vacation, he might have recovered; but he still continued his studies. His college were so gratified with his diligence, that they offered him a private tutor during the long vacation—a fatal gift, as this only incited him to exertions which his strength could not bear. To his own relatives he continued to write hopefully; but a letter to a friend reveals a different tale: there he speaks of palpitations, and nights of horror; how he could not bear to be alone, but craved for society, which most of his friends, reading men like himself, were too occupied to give him. At the end of the long vacation, he came to London; but the excitement of the metropolis did him harm, and he went back to college completely broken down in health. A few days after the commencement of term, his brother was summoned to him; but he was then delirious. The dying student recognised him but for a few moments, and sank into a stupor; and on Sunday, October 19, 1806, his spirit departed.

Thus died, at the early age of twenty-one years, the victim of his own excessive diligence, one of the finest spirits that the University of Cambridge, rich in a noble roll of men known to fame, ever received into her bosom. Would that a more discriminating use of the noble talents committed to him had induced him to spare his strength! for had it been more carefully husbanded, it may be the world and the Church also should have had more fruit of them. But who can refrain from sympathising with the struggles of this brilliant and earnest man? If White were wrong in not listening to his mother's remonstrances,—and that he was wrong, none can doubt, —still it was a disobedience which had in it something noble and sublime. A university scholarship is an honour which conquering veterans in the walks of literature or science look back upon as not the least worthy of their triumphs. No wonder that White pursued even too eagerly the glorious prize. Beside, in his case, there was added to the inducements of emulation strong enough to incite those to exertion who have in wealth all that heart could wish, the necessity of obtaining his daily subsistence. In his case, university distinction meant not only fame, but bread. He was swimming in deep waters, and he strove so against the adverse stream as to die of exhaustion just as he reached the shore. If he be a warning to a few ardent spirits not to tax their strength too far,—a warning sometimes needed,—to very many he is an example of diligence which, if it were more extensively imitated, though it might not make dunces into poets, would transform many idle students into industrious scholars.

His character as a man and a Christian stood deservedly high. Indeed, his patrons were such more on the ground of his piety than of his talents. From Mr. Simeon and his college tutor, Mr. Catton, he received fatherly kindness. The latter, no doubt unaware how dangerously his health had been broken by excessive application, aggravated the mischief by the offer of that help in his studies which would have tended, under ordinary circumstances, to diminish his burden. Simeon, we may be sure, thought more of the piety of his pupil than of his poetry,—and rightly: his poetry is like the immature bud or green fruit which tells us what, had it ever been gathered, the harvest would have been; but his piety was already mature. Irritability and youthful pride had disappeared; it was impossible for man to be more tenderly patient of the faults of others, more uniformly meek, more unaffectedly humble, than he was; and if he subtracted unduly from hours which would have been more wisely given to recreation or sleep, he never allowed his reading to trench on those given to devotion. If he did not obtain the earthly laurels, because he did not strive lawfully, we cannot doubt that faith unfeigned like his has entered into that glory which is incorruptible, undefiled, and fadeth not away.

The following fragment appears to be almost the last piece of poetry he wrote—the subject being the Saviour's life:

"Thus far have I pursued my solemn theme;
With self-rewarding toil, thus far have sung
Of godlike deeds, far loftier than beseem
The lyre which I, in early days, have strung,
And now my spirit faints, and I have hung
The shell, that solaced me in saddest hour,
On the dark cypress, and the strings which rung
With Jesu's praise; their harpings now are o'er,
Or, when the breeze comes by, moan, and are heard no more.

And must the harp of Judah sleep again?
Shall I no more reanimate the lay?
O Thou who visitest the sons of men,
Thou who dost listen when the humble pray,
One little lapse suspend Thy last decree,—
I am a youthful traveller in the way,
And this slight boon would consecrate to thee,
Ere I with Death shake hands, and smile that I am free."

This beautiful and touching fragment reveals to us plainly the faith in which he died, though the over-cloudings of delirium prevented, at his very last moments, any expression of it. He was ready for his departure; yet, as was natural in one called away so young, he casts "one longing, lingering look behind."

EDWARD IRVING, THE ENTHUSIAST.

Faith in Credulity.

"If in so great variety of ways as the wit of man is easily able to find out towards any purpose, and in so great liking as all men especially have unto those inventions whereby some one shall seem to have been more enlightened from above than many thousands, the Church did give every man license to follow what himself imagineth that God's Spirit doth reveal unto him, or what he supposeth that God is likely to have revealed to some special person whose virtues deserve to be highly esteemed, what other effect could hereupon ensue but utter confusion in His Church, under pretence of being taught, led, and guided by His Spirit?"—HOOKER, *Ecc. Pol.* v. 11.

LIFE OF EDWARD IRVING, THE ENTHUSIAST.

N the little Scotch town of Annan, near the Solway Firth, on the 4th of August 1792, was born Edward Irving, the second son of Gavin Irving and Mary his wife. His father was a tanner—a respectable, well-to-do man. His mother, who was the ruling spirit of the household, was a fine, dark, high-spirited Scotchwoman, whose handsome features survived, it is said, in the person of her son. Of his early childhood little is recorded; and no event of interest occurred, except a narrow escape from drowning. The Solway is a broad arm of the sea at high water; but when the tide is out, it meanders, diminished to a tenth of its magnitude, through vast banks of sand. The tide, however, rises with dangerous rapidity, and accidents to those who have strayed too far away from the high-tide line are not infrequent. It happened that

Edward and his elder brother John had gone down with the intention of meeting their uncle, George Lowther. They began fishing for such sea-monsters as frequent that shore, and in that interesting pursuit forgot both their uncle and the rising tide. While thus occupied, a man came up to them, galloping at full speed, who immediately seized on the astonished boys, and, throwing them across the horse's neck,—for he was a man of vast strength,—did not draw rein until they reached the shingle-bank; and then the boys found that it was their uncle—who, pointing back, showed them that the waves were pouring over the place where they had just before been standing.

At thirteen, Irving began his studies at Edinburgh University, accompanied by his brother John, who was destined for the medical profession. Nothing, it appears, can be more different than the methods and modes of university life north and south of the Tweed. The Scotch universities are but a mass of class-rooms, museums, and libraries; the youths, or rather boys, who seek instruction in them being under no university control or discipline whatever. On the other hand, they are,—or, at least, in Irving's time they were,—for the most part, really "poor scholars," who, with limited means, live hard in their solitary lodgings, and look to their learning as a means of livelihood, to be made available as speedily as possible: in many cases seeking, by tuition or otherwise, to earn something which may serve as a help in the expense of their own education.

The Edinburgh session only lasts from November to May, leaving the whole summer free as a vacation-time; or, more probably, for the labours of the self-supporting students, who thus are able to earn in vacation enough to support them during the months devoted specially to study. When these vacations arrived, the boys would send their boxes home by the carrier, and themselves walk, as the crow flies, across country to their home. In after years, Irving greatly delighted in such pedestrian excursions. In these walks, he would stop at the cottages on his way, and share with their poor inhabitants the potato or porridge he found there. This was afterwards of great service to him in his pastoral ministrations; he could enter the houses of the poorer members of his flock with a loving and lofty friendliness which gave dignity as well as entrance to his message.

At seventeen, he took his degree; but in Scotland the degree, in place of being, as in England, the passport to orders, is only the first stage. Four years are spent ere the degree is earned; but, after this, another four must be added, of special preparation for the ministerial office: and from four to six months in each of these four years are devoted to theology, Hebrew, ecclesiastical history, and other kindred studies. This very long and onerous course could not be borne by the comparatively slender means of the Irving family, without some extraneous assistance; and accordingly Edward did what almost all theological students are accustomed to do—began to help himself onwards during the interval by teaching. There was about to be established at Haddington a new school, called the "Mathematical;" and to this, with recommendations from Sir John Leslie, Irving was appointed master. He was then eighteen—a tall, ruddy, robust, handsome youth, cheerfully and kindly disposed. He soon won the confidence of his advanced pupils, and was admitted into the best society of the town and neighbourhood. As a schoolmaster, he was characteristically both severe and gentle: ruling with a discipline somewhat stern in school; out of it, the companion and friend of his scholars. At Haddington he remained two years. Thence he removed to Kirkaldy, a somewhat more important post, where he was attended with the same success as before. His scholars were attached to him, and playfully called themselves Irvingites—a name of very different import afterwards. Yet it appears that the careless and idle were treated with a little severity; sounds were sometimes heard which roused the indignant sympathy of the neighbours. It is said that, on one occasion, a carpenter, a man of great strength, entered the schoolroom, and, with an axe on his shoulder, and his shirt-sleeves turned up, ironically offered his assistance in the punishment department, with the words: "Do ye want a hand the day, Mr. Irving?"

One of his pupils at the school—for, according to the Scotch plan, boys and girls were taught together —was the eldest daughter of the parish-minister, Isabella Martin. Not long after she ceased to be a pupil, he became engaged to her. Her father, the Rev. John Martin, was a man of deep piety, belonging to the religious school which in Scotland was then called the "wild," or "highfliers," in opposition to the "moderates;" a distinction apparently similar to that which obtained south of the Tweed between "Evangelicals" and "High Church:" the "moderates" being, for the most part, so very moderate, that there was little of earnestness or devotion among them. There can be no doubt that the friendship with the high-flying minister, and his intimacy at the manse, had considerable influence in forming Irving's religious opinions; and, though these friends did not sympathise with him in those peculiar views which he held at the latter part of his life, they remained, nevertheless, firm friends to the last.

He had now completed his necessary college exercises, and was admitted to what, in the technical language of the Presbyterian Church, are called "trials for license." These endure half a year, and consist of various literary exercises, and a circular letter of inquiry into character, the object of which is to determine the candidate's fitness for the work of the ministry; and these proving satisfactory, he has a license to preach, but is not ordained until he receives a call, and has a flock of his own to which he may minister.

In this way, Irving was admitted, in the early part of the year 1815, to preach the Gospel; and "he exercised his gift," as the Scotch say, in Kirkaldy and other places, but with no great amount of success. The popular verdict was, that he had "ower muckle gran'ner." The good people of Kirkaldy had been used to a more plain and moderate style of preaching; and his lofty, and even turgid, eloquence flew over their heads. When, therefore, he officiated for Dr. Martin, there was a visible thinning of the congregation, who little appreciated the depth of thought and power of expression which the young preacher must even then have displayed, and which, with maturer judgment, and, it may be, deeper convictions, carried him, in after years, to an amazing popularity, though short-lived.

There is, indeed, no means of judging what was the real state of his religious convictions at this period of his life; and we cannot, therefore, affirm, though this is possible, that he failed to produce convictions in others, because, as yet, he had them not himself. There is no such record existing in his case, as we have found in other biographies, of that critical moment of conversion which forms the turning-point of the life. That in some way, and at some time, it must have taken place, we cannot doubt; but his was one of those spotless and blameless lives—

marred rather by defects of temper, and a certain lofty pride, than by what the world, at least, would call gross transgressions—a life in which there was no scope for a great and sudden outward change. If we judge of his opinions as they appear in his writings, we shall probably come to the conclusion that his spiritual life matured slowly, and was personally of a high type; but that this lofty spirituality and high idealism were combined with a defective judgment and love of the mystical, which would tend to leave him specially open to those errors into which he afterwards fell, and by which the closing scenes of his life were rendered so bitterly tragical.

In 1818, he left Kirkaldy: teaching had become irksome to him, and he was anxious for a settled ministry of his own. He spent the intervening time in Edinburgh, attending upon the classes there. He had thoughts of taking up the missionary work of the Church, and sailing westward, to carry the Gospel to shores where it was as yet unknown. It was while his mind was in suspense that he was invited by Dr. Andrews, minister of St. George's, Edinburgh, to preach in his church—the object being, apparently, to recommend him to the notice of Dr. Chalmers, who was in need of an assistant in Glasgow. He preached accordingly, and not without some slight success; but a considerable time elapsed, and he heard nothing more of Dr. Chalmers. In the interval, he again turned his thoughts to missionary enterprise; but apparently with the desire of further consideration, and perhaps, also, to occupy himself during a time of suspense and anxiety, he sailed in a small coasting-vessel to Belfast.

His Irish tour was accomplished, like his Scotch, on foot; walking as the crow flies, and finding shelter in the cabins of the peasantry. While in Ireland, Dr. Chalmers wrote, inviting him to go to Glasgow: but the date of the letter, by the time it reached Irving, was some weeks back; and, moreover, the object of the invitation was by no means distinct. But it revived Irving's failing spirit; he at once went to Glasgow, to find Dr. Chalmers absent, and thus to endure a still further period of suspense. Dr. Chalmers, on his return to Glasgow, proposed that he should become his assistant at St. John's. Irving assented, but, with characteristic humility, said: "I will preach to the people, if you think fit; but if they bear my preaching, they will be the first people who have borne with it." Thus he was ready to give up the position he so earnestly desired to fill, rather than be, as Presbyterians express it, "intruded" on an unwilling flock. He was, however, generally well liked; but some people thought him rather flowery. It was thus, with little confidence in himself, and with somewhat careless indulgence on the part of his hearers, that Irving first began a regular ministration; still, however, only as a candidate, or probationer,—for the flock was not his own.

At Glasgow, his success was rather that of a parish-priest than a preacher. The times were such as were enough to try the mettle of a pastor, and show clearly what manner of man he was. It was a period of commercial depression; work was slack, and there was much want. The Glasgow work-people, in their hunger, began to be seditious also, and risings were expected amongst them. It was the work of Chalmers and Irving to relieve this distress; and it was an especially favourable incident in the history of the commercial metropolis of the North, that it had the united services of two such men, so different and yet so at one, as Chalmers and Irving. The former appears as the statesman who could organise the machinery by which the destitution, both moral and spiritual, might be reached, the practical man who knows how to do it; the latter, his colleague, is not, and never could be, a practical man at all. He is an enthusiast; he is ready, in the homes, not over-clean or savoury, of the poor, starving mechanics of Glasgow, to minister the Gospel of the grace of God; and he enters them as a friend and a brother, with something of the lowliness of an equal, and yet with the lofty superiority of one who felt himself to be a messenger of the King of kings. Yet, when occasion served, he could command a certain noble craft, which, when men were inclined to resist, would catch them with guile. An instance is told of a radical and infidel cobbler, whose family was amongst those committed to Irving's special care. From him, Irving could elicit no response beyond a sullen "humph" of implied contempt, as he addressed his words to the trembling, almost deprecating, wife. One day, however, a piece of patent leather lying upon the bench formed an opening for discourse; Irving took it up, and remarked upon it in somewhat technical language. At first, the man worked on in sullen silence; but at length, exasperated by this apparent display of knowledge, he contemptuously asked, "What do ye ken about leather?" But Irving knew his duty to make all his studies draw one way; and accordingly he at once, as became a tanner's son, discoursed learnedly about that material. The shoemaker began to be interested; and thus a practicable breach was opened, at which, on a future occasion, other topics could be introduced. The man, also, was curious to hear how one who knew so much about leather could preach; and on the following Sunday he made an appearance at church. The next day, Irving met him, and they walked together along the street in friendly converse. The victory was complete: his children went to school, his wife to kirk, in peace; and he himself, in a suit of newly acquired "Sunday blacks," soon became a regular and constant attendant. His critique upon his new-found friend was characteristic: "He's a sensible man yon, for he kens about leather."

It must not be supposed, however, that this

knowledge of leather, and conversations about it, indicated that it was merely by earnest, cordial good-heartedness that the preacher won his way, discoursing of worldly things amidst his higher ministrations. He was himself, and he showed others that he was, deeply impressed with the solemnity of his office. As he entered a house, he would do so ever with the apostolic benediction, "Peace be to this house." This was pronounced to be "very peculiar, a thing nobody else did; it was impossible not to remark it, out of the way as it was: but there was not one of the agency [of visitors to the poor] who could make an objection to it; it took the people's attention wonderfully." And no marvel: it was no doubt felt to be genuine. The man came with a blessing in his heart, and so on his lips. In the same way, he would pronounce a blessing on each child of the house, laying his hand upon his head, and saying, "The Lord bless thee and keep thee." But though solemn, he was never cold; he would enter keenly into the domestic difficulties and sufferings of his people: he would give thanks over their homely fare, and, in brotherly fellowship, be not ashamed to partake of it. He had, indeed, little in his hand to give, but he gladly gave of that little, and, it is said, spent an unexpected legacy of some twenty pounds—it may have been a good deal more—in donations to those who needed amongst his flock. Thus it was, amidst the famishing multitudes of Glasgow, that he mitigated their sufferings with the bread of life. Expressed in his own verbose and laboured eloquence, it was, "that such application to the heart's ailments is there in our religion, and such a hold in its promises, and such a pith of endurance in its noble examples, that when set forth by our inexperienced tongue, with soft words and kindly tones, they did never fail to drain the heart of the sourness that calamity engenders, and sweeten it with the balm of resignation; often enlarge it with cheerful hope, sometimes swell it high with the rejoicings of a Christian triumph."

It was, then, thus ministered, that the Gospel obtained an entrance to the hearts of his people. It went from the heart to the heart, and in a measure his success was great. Yet only in a measure; for, with his preaching, matters remained much as before. When he had the duty, he would meet the disappointed crowds coming out of the sanctuary with disappointed looks, and the complaint, "It's no himsel' the day"—himself being Chalmers. It is true that it was no wonder that the substitute for Chalmers—then, perhaps, the most popular preacher of the time—should be coldly looked upon; and, though there is a certain strange family likeness in their style, they were, nevertheless, so different, that those who relished the preaching of the one, would hardly like that of the other. There were a few, indeed, who already had discovered that they had, if not a prophet, at least a preacher, among them; as yet, it was but a few.

Naturally enough, also, Irving longed for a flock of his own; without this, he could not be an ordained minister of his Church,—and to be ordained was what he most earnestly desired. He was even meditating anew the missionary field of work, when the call came which opened the way to the accomplishment of his desires. This was from the Caledonian Church in Hatton Garden, London. The congregation was diminishing, the situation obscure; but he was ready to take the charge; and he accordingly came up, the day before Christmas 1821, to make trial of his gifts before the remnant of the congregation which still held together. After various delays, all was at length satisfactorily settled, and Irving preached his farewell sermon at Glasgow. Thence he proceeded to his father's house at Annan; here his final "trials" for ordination were to take place. As he had been baptised in the church there, so did he desire that there he should have conferred upon him the solemn office of one of her ministers. And with bright hopes of future usefulness, and a determination to give scope to his aspirations after a higher style of preaching,—or, as he said, "to go deep into the ocean of truth,"—he journeyed southwards to his flock.

On the second Sunday in July 1822, Irving began his labours in London. The congregation consisted of the fifty persons who had signed his call, and their dependants; together with a few Scotchmen residing in London. By degrees, however, the little chapel began to fill. Soon after he was settled in his new cure, Dr. Chalmers preached a sermon for his late assistant, as is usual in the Presbyterian Church, commending him to his flock. The estimate of this great man is curious. "Mr. Irving, I left at Homerton," he writes to a friend; "and, as you are interested in him, I may say, once for all, that he is prospering in his new situation, and seems to feel as if in that very station of command and congeniality whereunto you have long known him to aspire. I hope that he will not hurt his usefulness by any kind of eccentricity or imprudence." The words were almost prophetic; but at present there were no signs of any dark cloud on the horizon of his hopes; all was bright and clear before him: he was, for a while, to have the success he most desired.

He had hardly been a year in London, when his chapel became crowded, and that with some of the most learned and noble personages of the day; who came all the way from the fashionable squares and terraces of the west to the dull precincts of Hatton Garden, in order to listen, with rapt attention, to the marvellous eloquence of the preacher. No one who reads his sermons will be surprised at this; they are remarkable enough, even when regarded as written compositions. Albeit, we may notice, by the way, that some of the sermons which have commanded the widest popularity cannot be *read*, and, when apart from the living voice by which they were delivered, seem utterly tame and commonplace. But not so with Irving; period after period of majestic and spirit-moving language flows on in one magnificent tide of thought and utterance. The expression is verbose and redundant, yet on that very account attractive, as each word adds a little to the thought. Thus the listener has time to meditate as the mind of the preacher unfolds; helped, rather than hindered, by the very redundancy of the words. Every thing, moreover, is expressed in the most lofty manner imaginable; the most commonplace matters being set forth in that kind of high ideal portraiture which sculptors affect, and by which they make an ordinary face and figure a colossal and majestic statue. Irving, indeed, succeeded in introducing the high style of preaching which he had so long dreamed of, and did plunge deep, only too deep, into the mysteries of God. He preached, moreover, to the learned and the critical; and for once, at least, they confessed that they had listened to sermons which were neither dull nor commonplace. To Irving himself, this was the realisation of his dearest hopes; he wished and desired to be nothing more than he was. He was bringing home, as he believed, to the great and learned of his people, that which he alone recognised as the everlasting wisdom; and he thanked his Lord that He had conferred so great an honour on His unworthy servant.

At this time he published his first book, *Orations*,

and the *Argument for Justice to come*, which rapidly reached a third edition; and thus took his place as a writer. This, also, was the year of his marriage. He had been engaged to Isabella Martin eleven years; and in September 1823 he left London for Kirkaldy. His reception in Scotland was very different to what it had been before; crowds now rushed to hear him preach: he was, indeed, fully and completely recognised as a pulpit-orator of no ordinary powers. With this bright prospect of fame and usefulness before him, and amidst much that augured the fulfilment of his highest hopes, he was united to his Isabella on the 13th of October, in the manse of Kirkaldy. Their hands were joined by the grandfather of the bride—for, as became such a one as Irving, his wife was by long descent a daughter of the sanctuary.

The bride and bridegroom hastened to their home in London, after a short marriage-trip, to enter into all the turmoil and excitement attendant on the life of a preacher so popular as Irving; and all the literary controversy which a writer so original, and at the same time so egotistical, was sure to provoke. But, though not unassailed by the angry voice of criticism, his career was a success. The little sanctuary in Hatton Garden had become too strait for so numerous a congregation as now attended it, and it was in contemplation to build another, handsomer and more commodious. This was afterwards accomplished in the erection of the church in Regent Square.

In May 1824, he was requested to preach the anniversary sermon of the London Missionary Society. Such a request was itself a high tribute to his popularity; and accordingly, not only the interest of the subject and the occasion, but also the popularity of the preacher, justified the expectation that a large and successful gathering would greatly promote the cause the Society had at heart.

Tottenham-Court-Road Chapel, originally erected for Whitefield, was the building chosen for the sermon, as possessing accommodation for a large audience. But long before the appointed time of service, though the day was wet and gloomy, the chapel was already crowded, and it was deemed advisable to commence the service a full hour sooner than had been originally intended. The sermon was inordinately long, lasting over three hours; but this was, by comparison, a small matter. The topic was the missionary after the apostolic school; and, in place of the prosaic details of an ordinary missionary sermon, the preacher described, in glowing language, his ideal of what a missionary ought to be—a man without scrip or purse, going, with burning lips, unflinching faith, and spotless holiness, to proclaim the message of salvation to a world which, though lying in wickedness, would be startled out of its iniquities by the very fervour and earnestness of the spirit of those that preached to it. The preacher seemed to rate at a very low estimate, and spoke almost contemptuously of, the modern machinery of missionary societies, with their calculating prudence and committee-rules, their salaries and subscription-lists,—these lesser efforts of modern times were but sparks of divine grace, which he hoped might prove to be the slender beginnings of better things. "The word of God," he said, "is at first a spark, then it is a burning coal, at length it is a consuming fire, within the hearts of His servants; and they are weary of forbearing, and cannot stay nor hold their peace; they must speak, or they must die: and though they should die, they will speak then. They have no rest, but hasten over land and sea, over rocks and trackless deserts. They cry aloud, and spare not, and will not be hindered. In the prisons they lift up their voices, and in the tempests of ocean they are not silent; before awful councils and throned kings they witness in behalf of the truth: nothing will quench their voice but death. And in the article of death, ere yet the spiry flame and rolling smoke have suffocated the organs of the soul, they speak, they pray, they testify, they confess, they beseech, they warn, and at length they bless the cruel people." Such was his description of the apostolic missionary; but it seemed to his audience that, in magnifying the ideal, he had depreciated the actual; and that he had, to a certain extent, injured the cause he came to advocate. Accordingly, the religious world was in a state of excitement. The secretary of the society wrote *An Expostulatory Letter*, which he published; and Irving, on his side, published his sermon, or rather the beginning of a work of which this sermon formed the introduction, intending to set forth his idea of missionary enterprise. The reasoning of this book is no doubt defective; and the writer, while happy enough in his expositions of those Scriptures which are on his own side, fails to see the bearing of others which do what Scripture ever does, combine the noblest and highest possible ideal of duty with the most perfect adaptation to human weakness and infirmities. But we must admit, considering all things, that the fathers of the London Missionary Society, remembering the character of the man with whom they had to deal, were a little unreasonable. The preacher was certainly right in this, that a cold, calculating, money-getting age is just that which needs most to have set before it such a high and lofty ideal; and it was no doubt a wholesome admonition which he had prepared for them, though perhaps a little out of season as an anniversary sermon of the society. This anniversary is looked upon in the light of a festival, and it was perhaps ill-judged to take that opportunity to set forth a portraiture of missionary zeal which must have sounded a good deal like a depreciation of the existing agencies. But Irving was a man of lofty ideas: he seldom thought of the practical; and to him it seemed strange that such a sermon should be received, as it was by his brethren, with distaste and disapproval.

While his work was in preparation, his eldest child was born, on July 22, 1824, and baptised as Edward by his great-grandfather, who on this occasion, with all his family about him, saw his children's children, even four generations. Little Edward was the pride of his father, or, as he expressed it, his excellency, and the beginning of his strength. It often happened that, in his walks with Mrs. Irving in the streets of Pentonville, where they now resided, the tall Scotch clergyman might be seen with the boy in his arms, not caring the least for the laughter which the strange spectacle sometimes excited in the by-standers. The child only lived a year, and his death was the first of those clouds which began to overshadow that happy home; but at present all was bright. The foundation-stone of his new church in Regent Square was laid, whilst his popularity and usefulness were undiminished. Those who visited his house were many of them men of high literary eminence, whose converse and friendship must have been especially delightful to him; these all bore testimony to the earnestness of his faith, confessing that he was one who in his Lord lived and moved and had his being—that his dwelling was one where no act was done but in prayer, every blessing was received with thanksgiving to God, every friend was dismissed with a parting benediction. Yet, with all this, he lost nothing of simplicity.

In the year 1825, he met with Mr. Hatley Frere, a prophetic student, who, however, could obtain little audience for his deliverances on that mysterious subject. Through this acquaintance, Irving was introduced to Mr. Drummond, at whose residence—Albury, in Surrey—he met with those who, from their studies in prophetic Scripture, were known as the "Albury Prophets." This is not the place in which the writer can enter into any discussion on a topic so important as the manner in which prophetic Scripture should be studied, and why it is that Irving and his followers erred, as the writer believes them to have done. Irving's book on the Revelation—which, published some time afterwards, may be considered as containing his mature judgment on the subject—has all the faults of his other writings, and less, perhaps, of that eloquence and sublimity which we find elsewhere. He is not so happy in illustrating and explaining the Scriptures on his own side; he fails more than is his wont to see the force of those that make against him. His treatise, moreover, is in the form of lectures delivered to a congregation. Now, it is not too much to say that this is the most unfavourable form possible for such a work. The most minute and patient criticism of every word is necessary in order to understand a book which every where alludes to, if it does not quote, earlier prophecies; and this Irving has not done—it was beside his purpose to do it: and yet we venture to affirm that without it not even the initial step can be taken in prophetic interpretation. The introduction to Mr.

Frere was a turning-point in Irving's life, which opened the way to those opinions that he held afterwards, and which caused so great a stir in the Church.

But we must return to his domestic life. Little Edward was seized with whooping-cough, and, late in June, was taken by his mother—herself in delicate health — to Kirkaldy, for change of air. Irving remained in town. In the September, he went northward to join his wife, who was expecting the birth of their second child. The pleasant summer weather had restored both mother and child; but with the autumn winds came a change. The child sickened again, and in a few weeks began visibly to draw near his end. Ten days after the birth of his sister, who was baptised Margaret, he died in the arms of his father, to his great grief. Yet he could write to a friend and member of his congregation: "I feel that the Lord hath done well, that He hath afflicted me, and that by His grace I shall be a more faithful minister unto you, and unto all the flock committed to my charge. Now is my heart broken, now is its hardness melted, and my pride is humbled, and my spirit renewed. The good name of the Lord be praised!" Thus we perceive that Irving had that spirit of consolation which all God's servants possess.

The church in Regent Square was now complete, and early in 1827 was opened, Chalmers preaching the opening sermon. Irving on this occasion, with a characteristic want of tact, allowed the preliminary services to extend to the length of an hour and a half. This was hardly fair to Chalmers; for, though the services of the Church of God are not so to be regulated that popular preachers may display their eloquence, it was clearly not to edification to keep people waiting so long. Chalmers also notices that Irving preached on "his prophecies" for two hours and a half; and, although very powerful, yet the people were dropping away. "I fear," says he, "lest his prophecies, and the excessive length and weariness of his services, may unship him altogether; and I mean to write to him seriously on the subject."

The great Scotch preacher was right. This inordinate length of service was one cause which undermined Irving's popularity,—for about this time it was evident that his popularity had begun to diminish. The church at Regent Square was opened, and, though usually well filled, was no longer crowded. If he had indulged in visions of a ministry which should evangelise all London, he was clearly about to be disabused altogether,—he was the pastor of a large and important congregation, and that was all. "Fashion," says a biographer, "had gone her idle way." There is no reason, however, to believe that to Irving this was a special disappointment, or that he in any wise loved his popularity for its own sake. If he felt the difference at all, he would only feel it as a difference in the amount of his usefulness, which, as he must have been well aware, depended principally on his own power as a preacher. He never had, apparently,—it was quite alien to his nature,—the design, or even the desire, to organise a sect or party, even though in the result there be one which is sometimes called by his name.

The truth is, that, notwithstanding their immense power, his sermons suffer by the excessive preponderance of doctrinal statement. Underneath can always be discerned the beatings of the warm, earnest, loving Christian heart; but above this are the coruscations of an intellect which dazzles, and sometimes confounds, by its array of metaphor and arguments. His beautiful and touching sermons on the death of infants, elicited from him by his own loss of his infant Mary, contain an elaborate statement of the doctrine of baptismal regeneration. With him, earnest piety is wedded to what is termed, perhaps somewhat disrespectfully, "Scotch metaphysics." How, with such topics as he discussed, he had a congregation at all, is a mystery which is only partially explained by the fact that its nucleus consisted of hard-headed Scotchmen. And it was in this excessive love of dogma that his troubles commenced. He had preached and published a series of sermons on the Incarnation. He was declared by his theological opponents to have stated in them the doctrine of Christ's sinful human nature. It appears that a Mr. Cole, a Church-of-England clergyman, was the first to lead the attack; and this was followed up by members of his own community. Who was right, and who was wrong, in this controversy, can hardly be discussed in a work like the present; but, as we shall see, the final result was disastrous. There can, indeed, be no doubt that, in the main, the judgment of Chalmers was correct. Speaking of a sermon, in a course of twelve upon the Apocalypse, he writes: "For the first time heard Mr. Irving. I have no hesitation in saying, it is quite woful. There is power and richness and gleams of exquisite beauty, but withal a mysterious and extreme allegorisation, which I am sure must be pernicious to the general cause." Prodigious crowds, nevertheless, attended these lectures, although held at the unseasonable hour of six in the morning, attracted by these gleams of exquisite beauty; but they did no permanent good to the cause—of Christ's Church.

An incident may here be related, tending the same way; though it could have no permanent effect on his popularity. He had gone northwards, and, amongst other engagements,—one of which was the Apocalyptic lectures referred to above,—agreed to preach in Kirkaldy Church on the Sunday evening on which the communion was administered, and which coincided with his own wedding-day. A prodigious crowd gathered in Kirkaldy Church, and the galleries, not able to sustain the unusual weight, fell, just before the service was about to begin. Only two or three persons were killed by the actual fall of the galleries, but a panic commenced in the crowded building. As many as twenty persons were killed by suffocation, or were trodden to death in the rush that ensued. Irving immediately took up his post under a window, and, conspicuous for his great size and strength, lifted many down in his arms. It is clearly no part of the duty of a strange preacher to test the strength of the building in which he is about to officiate, and no possible blame could rest upon Irving. Nevertheless, the public wanted its usual victim, and seemed inclined to fix upon Irving. He, on his side, felt bitterly the accident, happening, as it did, amidst the scenes of his early friendship, in the church of his father-in-law. "God," he said, "hath put me to shame this day before all the people."

We have already noticed, also, Irving's acquaintance with Mr. Drummond and the Albury school of prophets, of whose annual conference he was a diligent and honoured member; but it is easy to see that such studies would do him no good. There is much more of the show of reason in Irving's works than the reality. He could convince both himself and friends by arguments apparently irrefutable, but which nevertheless often beg the whole question at issue. Accordingly, he persuaded himself that he had obtained a complete insight into the mysteries of prophecy, and that there lay, as it were, mapped out before him, a complete chart of the future of the Church. A mistake as to the meaning of an unfulfilled prophecy might not have been of great consequence, as the event would vindicate the correct interpretation; but the habit of speculation thus engendered was especially dangerous to a man of Irving's temperament. He was thus ready, so soon as they should be presented to him in a sufficiently specious form, to be misled by supposed manifestations from the invisible world; and he was incapable of examining into the evidence of such manifestations in a sufficiently impartial spirit. The way in which he became subject to this delusion forms a remarkable chapter in the history of religious enthusiasm.

Since the summer of 1828, Mr. Alexander Scott, who is described as a man of some considerable powers, had been with him as a fellow-labourer in his Church, and exercised considerable influence over him. Irving, at this time, held the opinion that those spiritual gifts which appertained to the primitive Church might be exercised in these days, were there faith enough existing in the Church; but that, through this lack of faith, they were kept in abeyance, to be manifested again in the millennial Church. Mr. Scott held a more questionable, but more consistent, doctrine—that such gifts were the possession of the Church in all ages, and therefore might be expected to be vouchsafed at once, if she were found acting up to her privileges. Irving, convinced by his friend's arguments, came over to his views, though as yet, he declares, "I was still little moved to seek myself, or stir up my people to seek, these spiritual treasures." Yet, he adds, "I went forward to contend and to instruct, whenever the subject came before me in my public ministrations of reading and preaching the Word, that the Holy Ghost ought to be manifested among us all, the same as ever He was in any one of the primitive Churches."

That Irving was wrong is, we think, manifest from the following considerations. The miracle is ever worked, not for the sake of the natural effect, but as a sign to the Church; and the more reasonable and Scriptural doctrine we believe to be, that such manifestations are vouchsafed, not so much in regard to the faith of the Church, but in regard to her needs; and that the gifts of the Spirit which may be expected in answer to prayer will be those which, at that time and in those circumstances, will most conduce to edification and advancement. In other words, this expectation of the miraculous was, on the part of Irving and his followers, to a certain extent, a practical overlooking of the immediate providential presence of God—an attempt, however little they might recognise it as such, to walk by sight, and not by faith.

At this time, also, Irving was involved still further in the controversy to which we have already alluded concerning our Lord's human nature. At present, he was not the principal; Mr. Scott and Mr. Maclean, who had been minister of the Scotch Church in London Wall, were the first to fall under the charge of heresy. Mr. Scott had received a call to the Church at Woolwich, and Mr. Maclean a presentation to a living in Ayrshire. The necessary legal formalities to which this change in their sphere of ministrations gave rise, afforded an opening for the formal discussion of the doctrine which they held in common with Irving; and the question of his and their orthodoxy was thus formally brought before the General Assembly.

While all this was proceeding, with the usual bitterness attending theological controversy,—which, it seems, loses none of its bitterness on the other side of the Tweed,—and the consequent agitation of mind on the part of Irving, who, with characteristic one-sidedness, looked upon his own statement of the doctrine of the Incarnation in a special form as the very essence of Christianity, there came tidings that miraculous gifts had been manifested in the person of a Mary Campbell, who lived at Fernicarry, at the head of Gairloch. Isabella Campbell, the elder sister of Mary, who appears to have been a person of remarkable earnestness and piety, had recently died. During her lifetime, she had been visited by the country round almost as a medieval saint might have been; and, now she was gone, her mantle seemed to have descended on her sister Mary. Yet Mary also seemed to be about to follow her sister; for symptoms of decline, the disease of which Isabella died, had already manifested themselves,—and she was, to all appearance, drawing near her end. "It was," writes Irving, who describes the circumstance, "on the Lord's Day; and one of her sisters, together with a female friend, who had come to the house for that end, had been spending the whole day in humiliation and fasting and prayer, with a special respect to the restoration of the gifts. They had come up in the evening to the sick-chamber of their sister, who was laid on a sofa, and, along with one or two others of the household, they were engaged in prayer together. It was while in prayer together that Mary Campbell was constrained to speak at great length, and with superhuman strength, in an unknown tongue." It was thus that the manifestation of the "tongues" began—and began, no doubt, in good faith; but we must not fail to notice that the beginning of these manifestations was after a long interval of fasting and prayer, when an excitable person would be especially open to that kind of religious impression, under the influence of which she might well mistake emotion for inspiration. So different this to the calm, self-possessed manifestation of the Day of Pentecost,—in which, amongst other things, we ought thankfully to notice the apparently unimportant incident, that it took place before the third hour of the day. It is, indeed, very necessary to look these facts in the face, in order that we may estimate aright the real nature of such a movement, and the true character of those engaged in it. When once such a manifestation had been experienced, and traced to a supernatural influence, it would not be easy to discredit it. The earnest would deceive themselves, as well as be deceived, and deal as unfairly with their own reasonings as we shall see they did with those of others.

But this was not all. Mary Campbell still remained apparently in a dying state; but was suddenly cured, and that by a miracle. On the opposite shore of the Clyde, in Port Glasgow, lived two brothers, James and George Macdonald, ship-builders; men in the position of ordinary workmen. They had a sick sister, who was the subject of this manifestation. At dinner-time, the brothers came home from work as usual. The sister begged that they would pray at that time for the manifestation of the Spirit. Suddenly James said: "I have it." He then walked to his sister's bed-side, and said: "Arise, and stand upright." He said this again, took her by the hand, and the young woman arose, it is said, completely cured. On this, James Macdonald sent a letter to Mary Campbell, then apparently approaching death, commanding her also to arise. On the receipt of the letter, she immediately arose from her bed, and declared herself cured, and, without any interval, returned to an active life. This strange circumstance attracted more attention than ever. She was visited by vast numbers; and she entered into the career of a gifted person, expounding and giving utterances of her power in crowded assemblies.

The matter soon began to attract attention beyond the limits of her village, and several clergymen and persons of education began to inquire; even Chalmers would not hastily condemn. Irving, however, was less cautious: he could not doubt of the piety and earnestness of those in whom these gifts were manifested, and was ready to accept them as a real outpouring of the Spirit. Nor was this to be wondered at. His own teaching for a long time tended this way; and, however weak his arguments may be, no one can read his discourses without feeling that the author is fully persuaded in his own mind. Harassed, also, by the doctrinal controversies around him, he would hail such an occurrence as a precious gift of consolation to a warring and suffering Church.

But, if Irving was deceived, he was never a deceiver—not even unconsciously, and in good faith. None of these so-called miraculous gifts came to him. His little daughter Mary at this time was evidently dying; but no prophetic voice conveyed to him the tidings of relief, no gifted person could send letters which should restore the infant's life. The child died late in the week; and there was no time to obtain help for the Sunday. Accordingly, he preached the two sermons next Sunday on the "Death of Children;" and elaborately reasons out, in the morning sermon, the doctrinal use of such events to the Church. In the evening, the sermon was more of a personal character, and the suffering father is not altogether out of sight; yet no one who simply reads the published sermons could possibly anticipate the real state of the case. It is said that Irving went tearless and fasting all the day; and, coming in from his pulpit, went straight to the little coffin, and, flinging himself down, gave way to an agony of grief, mingled with prayers to the Lord for faith and patience—that Lord who had not, in his case, interposed to save.

In the mean time, the London Presbytery condemned his book; but Irving, considering that he had been ordained in Scotland, refused to submit to their jurisdiction. In this determination he was supported by his own Kirk Session. Nevertheless, the step he thus took virtually separated him from his Church; and he now stood alone, without the restraints which such a character specially needed.

At this time, the General Assembly of the Church of Scotland was about to meet. Irving instituted a prayer-meeting, which met at half-past six in the morning, for the express purpose of praying that the Assembly might be guided aright in their decisions. It is especially to be observed, that one of the deliverances of this Assembly was directed against Irving himself. A motion was made and carried, that if at any time the Rev. Edward Irving should claim the privilege of a licentiate or minister of the Church of Scotland, the Presbytery of the bounds should be enjoined to inquire whether he were the author of certain works, and that they should proceed thereafter as they should see fit. At the same time, Scott and Maclean were also dealt with. This was the first authoritative censure pronounced upon him.

When the session of the Assembly was over, the devout company of worshipers in the Scotch Church determined to continue their prayer-meeting. This time, they agreed to petition for a renewal of the gifts of the Spirit; and, to the apprehension of those who supplicated, this gift was at length vouchsafed,—at first privately, then in the comparative seclusion of the prayer-meeting, and last of all in the public congregation.

Irving was strongly prepossessed with the supernatural character of these manifestations. He had, as leader of the congregation, been earnestly praying for these gifts of the Spirit; and, as he says, with characteristic one-sided interpretation of Scripture, "I dared not believe that, when we had asked bread, He gave a stone; when we had asked fish, He gave a serpent:" thus assuming that his prayer, if granted, must be granted in that very form and manner in which he, in his short-sighted ignorance, had presented his petition, and not, as might have been the case, in invisible outpourings of the Spirit into the hearts of the members of his flock, thus leading them to greater enlightenment, deeper affection, and more earnest lives,—for this, and not the visible manifestation of an external power, was most to be desired. No doubt, in all sincerity, he "tried the spirits;" but he was not in a frame of mind to come to a safe conclusion. Honesty of purpose is not the only thing required in such investigations; one ought to have soundness of judgment: but this was sadly lacking. Had there been more of this, Irving might have discerned that, like many before his time, he had been led astray by mere spiritual emotion.

The form in which the " tongues" appeared was a strange outburst or crash of sound, apparently without meaning, followed by words of exhortation in English. The person uttering these tongues was usually observed to be in a state of considerable excitement. A Mr. Pilkington—who was a diligent attendant on these meetings, and at first a believer, but who afterwards wrote a pamphlet, entitled, *The Unknown Tongues discovered to be English, Spanish, and Latin; and the Rev. Ed. Irving proved to be erroneous in attributing their utterance to the influence of the Holy Spirit*—has preserved some of these utterances. He was accused, indeed, of being a needy man, who put his paper together in order to catch the market at the time when the " tongues" were producing a great popular excitement; but a careful perusal of his and a similar pamphlet by Mr. Baxter leads the author to the conviction that the matter can be explained without any recourse to supernatural agency at all. An utterance which Mr. Pilkington preserves is: " Gthis dil emma sumo." Strange as these words appear in this form, they are really only broken English. They occurred at a meeting of the gifted persons and their followers, at which Mr. Pilkington was present; and at which the question was under discussion, whether or no the Church should allow these utterances in the general congregation. They were uttered by a gifted sister, whose mouth shook and lips were stiffened with excitement. They are, no doubt, part of the sentence, "This dilemma will assume—" Another sitting may be described a little more at length. There was a service, with a psalm, prayer, and then a silence; a gifted sister then suddenly uttered the words: "Hozeghin alta stare;" and concluded, in English, that the Spirit should speak in the congregation. There was then a silence. Another sister uttered: "Holemole holif awthaw:" and finished, in English, to the same effect as the other. Then the first sister spoke again in the tongue, "Hozehamenanostra;" and then said in English, "Jesus will take care of us." The utterance of the second sister, Pilkington explains as being the words: "Holy, most holy Father." He has recourse to the Latin and Spanish languages, however, to interpret the mysterious sounds uttered by the first sister; but the words, "Jesus cannot at all stray; Jesus, the Amen, has not strayed," uttered very rapidly, and with the mouth open, are far more probable explanations, especially as there appears to be not the slightest evidence that these ladies understood either Latin or Spanish. According to his own account, this attempt on the part of Pilkington to interpret was very coldly treated indeed. The gifted persons, perhaps for the very reason that they were suspicious of themselves, rejected the attempt to translate their utterances as being imperfect recollections of known languages. "How," they asked, begging the very question at issue, "could the words of the Spirit be interpreted otherwise than by the Spirit?" Irving himself, who throughout appears the most sensible, as well as the most kind and courteous, of the party, was inclined to listen to reason; but the arguments of the others prevailed, and he was easily convinced of that which he wished to be true. It must be admitted, however, that there can be no suspicion of fraud. The gifted persons were all living holy and blameless lives, and had nothing to gain, and every thing to lose, by the delusion; but of their judgments we may very well doubt. Besides, there is something very soothing to the pride of human nature in the conviction that one is exalted above one's fellows by spiritual illumination—a kind of spiritual pride which even an Apostle needed a special "thorn in the flesh" to keep in subjection. We need not, then, doubt in the slightest degree of the earnestness and piety of Irving; but his judgment was very defective. Ideal and unpractical, he fell into the snare; and the consequences of his error were not a little disastrous both to himself and the Church he served.

While the tongues were confined to the prayer-meetings, they caused little excitement outside. But the case was very different when they first appeared in the congregation. This took place as follows: A sister (we notice how constantly women were the subjects of this influence), finding she was unable to restrain herself, rushed into the vestry. "The sudden doleful and unintelligible sounds being heard by all the congregation, produced the utmost confusion. The act of standing up, the exertion to hear and see and understand, in a congregation of 1500 to 2000 persons, created a noise which may be easily conceived." Irving, however, when order was restored, explained the occurrence, which, he said, was not new, except in the congregation, where he had been for some time considering the propriety of introducing it, being afraid of dispersing his flock; but now, as it was brought forward by God's will, he felt it his duty to submit. He then changed the subject of his sermon, expounding 1 Cor. xiv. Thus the morning service passed off. In the evening, a prodigious crowd was assembled, with the usual proportion of roughs and pickpockets to foment the disturbance, and profit by it. All was quiet until, at the end of the sermon, a gifted brother cried out, with a crash of tongues: "God is amongst us; and if you fly from Him now, where will you fly in the day of judgment?" This caused a rush; but Irving had presence of mind enough to still the multitude: and, though there was great danger, the people were induced to go away quietly at length, and no harm was done. During the week, Irving hesitated, and declared that he would not permit a repetition of the disturbance; but, himself convinced of the supernatural character of the tongues, before the next Sunday he retracted, and allowed the matter to take its course. As an honest man, he could hardly have done otherwise.

His friends and relations remonstrated with him, but without effect; he was thoroughly persuaded that these utterances were an immediate manifestation of the power and presence of the Divine Spirit. He took order, also, for a pause in the services, that the prophets might speak and edify the Church by their ministrations. The trustees of the Church were, however, unconvinced, and considered it their duty to put in action the clause in their trust-deed which gave them an appeal to the Presbytery of London. That this should be the body charged with the decision of this question was peculiarly unfortunate. Irving had denied their authority over him as a minister; and what court was ever known to be lenient to those who defied its authority? But the result, whatever the court of appeal, could hardly have been different. Thus the shadows began to darken around him. All the time, his own relatives plied him with arguments and remonstrances, beseeching him to give up these unreasonable and dangerous doctrines, as they appeared to them. He answered,—and the answer displays at once the strength and weakness of his character,—"There is nothing which I would not surrender to you, even to my life;" but he could not grant what his friends so urgently desired. He was convinced, on very weak grounds, it is true, and with probably some—though quite unconscious—self-deception, that these utterances were divine; and, being convinced, his duty required that he should sacrifice all—and he did not shrink. He was shut out of his pulpit, he was excommunicated by his Church, his friends forsook him. He himself was never the subject of those manifestations which he so confidently believed in and ardently desired; but he never could be induced to discredit, much less to silence, that voice which he believed was the voice of God.

Matters rapidly proceeded to extremity; the trustees of the Church submitted an opinion to counsel as to the legality, under the powers conferred in their deed, of permitting these utterances. The opinion was against Irving; and a deputation of the trustees was appointed to wait upon him, with the opinion in their hands. This is his answer: "I have read over the opinion of Sir Ed. Sugden. . . . The principle on which I have acted is to preserve the integrity of my ministerial character unimpaired, and to fulfil my office according to the word of God. If the trust-deed do fetter me therein, I knew it not when the trust-deed was drawn, and am sure that it never was intended in the drawing of it; for certainly I would not, to possess all the churches of this land, bind myself one iota from obeying the great Head and Bishop of the Church. But if it be so that you, the trustees, must act to prevent me and my flock from assembling to worship God according to the word of God in the house committed into your trust, we will look unto our God for preservation and safe keeping. Farewell! May the Lord have you in His holy keeping!"

The controversy was, in fact, hopeless: the trustees believed that Irving was under a delusion, and could only regard the tongues as a scandal and difficulty, to be got rid of without delay from the Church of which they were the trustees; Irving, on his side, believed that he was only doing his simple duty as a minister of the Gospel. The trial before the Presbytery came on in due course, and the result was just what might have been expected. The real point at issue, though necessarily to a great extent kept out of sight, was whether these manifestations were what Irving believed them to be; and the court, in effect, decided that they were not. They were glad to avoid any further question, for how otherwise could they escape making an imputation of fraud in these gifted ones?

The decision was still further influenced by the recantation of Mr. Robert Baxter. That gentleman had been one of the prophets, and had uttered predictions which had been falsified by the event. He was too honest a man not to be startled by so suspicious a circumstance, and was led to suspect that he had prophesied out of his own heart, when he had seen nothing. He came up the day before the trial to London, in order to expose the delusion to which he believed himself to be subject. Such a testimony, at such a juncture, was conclusive; and, to the writer's mind, who has carefully read his narrative afterwards published, decides the real question at issue. Baxter, indeed, does not deny spiritual influence in the matter, and attributes his delusions to an express intervention of the evil one. That the devil had deceived him, is apparent enough; but, after all, only by the ordinary enticements of spiritual pride and self-conceit. Baxter was, for a time, a leader among the prophets themselves; his utterances much more definite and precise than theirs—which latter, certainly, appear very like diluted and tautological amplifications of well-known scriptural denunciations: and he was proportionately honoured for what seemed his superior light, but was in reality his greater boldness and self-assertion. Irving, however, was too infatuated now to listen to the pleadings, however earnest, of his former disciple; and Baxter had the mortification of finding the most sincere recantation powerless to enlighten those who had been deceived by a self-deceiver: a circumstance too common in the history of the Church,—for many a heresy has survived after the heretic himself has most sincerely recanted.

The public press sang pæans of delight, the worldly papers discussed the matter from their worldly point of view, the so-called religious ones indulged in the usual amount of sanctimonious spite. It so turned out that the Sunday after the judgment of the Presbytery was Communion-Sunday, and an additional vexation to Irving must it have been to be inhibited from his church on that very day; but the trustees, possibly in some measure excused by the legal exigencies of their position, at once proceeded to prevent Irving from officiating, and the communion announced and prepared for was never administered. To this was added another blow. The inhibition was served on Thursday, and accommodation had to be sought for that large number of members which still adhered to Irving. No place was open to them except a large room in Gray's-Inn Road, occupied in the week-days by Robert Owen, the Socialist. Nothing could be more repugnant to the judgment, taste, and feelings of the members, than the asylum to which they were driven; "a barn or a cow-shed would have been preferable, but none such was to be obtained." And so the believers in a present and immediate influence of supernatural manifestation in the Church shared the room with sentimental unbelief. The congregation, amounting to about 800 communicants, assembled on May 6th; and thus, in this humble way, commenced the operations of the new sect,—most of them, we cannot doubt, firm believers in those gifts which, if indeed they had been what they supposed them to be, would have made the room in the dingy locality of Gray's-Inn Road of more honour than the stateliest cathedral.

The year in which all this happened was a remarkable one in the history of England. It was the year of the Reform Bill, which it was felt by all would make, for good or ill, a vast change in the constitution of England,—as, in truth, has come to pass; though we, in 1869, are almost as much in the dark as to the final result as they were then. At this time, also, the country was visited by the first epidemic outbreak of cholera. This pestilence, always terrible enough, was then strange and unknown, and great was the consternation as it passed in its mysteriously capricious way from street to street,—"one taken and another left." No wonder, then, that men's minds were excited, and that some thought that they possessed visible intimations of that Advent which they believed would immediately appear.

Irving was himself seized with the mysterious complaint. The attack, though severe, was not attended with the more fatal and exhausting symptoms. He, however, regarded sickness as mysteriously caused by sin, and had recourse to none but spiritual remedies. He determined to preach as usual, in firm faith that he should be healed. At first, as he confesses, the words dropped from him slowly, and in great weakness; but the effort of will proved beneficial, and the paroxysm of the disease passed away. To Irving this appeared something miraculous; yet it contrasts strongly with really miraculous histories, in which we find that the cure was complete, and strength was at once given. But he was, by this time, too deeply involved in the toils of his own enthusiasm to escape, and invested with a specially miraculous character an ordinary incident in the history of disease.

Meanwhile, the Church in Gray's-Inn Road received fresh revelations at the hands of its prophets; and thus was ultimately developed a gorgeous and elaborate ritual, as far distant from the severity of Scotch Presbyterianism as can well be imagined. The most important change, however,—a change which led to great difficulties and perplexities,—was that which substituted, in place of the law of the Church, the utterances, often fragmentary, of the prophets; and these difficulties were further complicated by the fact that even the members of the Church themselves were unable in all cases to distinguish between the utterance of false and true spirits. Thus it came to pass that sometimes "prophets" were at variance with "apostles," and that which was supposed, on apparently good ground, to be spoken in the "power," was not only falsified by the event, but even divine commands communicated by prophets were forbidden to be executed by some superior officer in the Church; it being alleged that the prophets had, in reality, been deceived by their own imaginings. Irving's position—if we may credit the accounts which have come down to us—was not a happy one. He was too fervent and simple-hearted a believer to tamper with prophecies, as his fellows were ready to do; and so it seems that his faith unconsciously acted as a kind of *reductio ad absurdum* of his principles. He was like a chemist amongst alchemists,—his balance too delicate to be deceived by their crude and hap-hazard experiments. If all his fellows had been as honest as himself, it is questionable if the delusion would have proceeded; for it is to be observed that, though the chief *Angel* of the Church, he was never endowed with the gift,—as he himself says, he was never found "worthy."

The Church of Scotland determined to cast out a man who now really belonged to her no more than in name; and a request from the General Assembly was sent to the Presbytery of Annan, to take order in regard to Irving's book concerning the humanity of our blessed Lord. Accordingly, Irving was cited before that court, and ostensibly the decision turned upon the doctrine as stated in the books entitled *The Orthodox and Catholic Doctrine of our Lord's Human Nature*, *The Day of Pentecost*, and a paper in *The Morning Watch*. The proceedings terminated in the unanimous decision of his judges that he was guilty of heresy, and he was accordingly deprived. The concluding scene was characteristic. The Moderator was about to proceed with the solemn duty of declaring the sentence, and, as a preliminary, requested Mr. Sloan, the senior member of the Presbytery, to offer up a prayer to Almighty God; when a voice was heard exclaiming: "Arise, depart! arise, depart! Flee ye out! flee ye out of her! Ye cannot pray! How can ye pray? how can ye pray to Christ, whom ye deny? Ye cannot pray! Depart, depart! Flee, flee!" The words proceeded from a Mr. Dow, one of the gifted persons. Mr. Dow rose, and with him Irving, who, with great vehemence, cried to the crowd, who somewhat obstructed his passage: "Stand forth! stand forth! What! will ye not obey the voice of the Holy Ghost? As many as will obey the voice of the Holy Ghost, let them depart." Irving, with his followers, then withdrew, and the sentence was passed which separated him from the Church in which he had been baptised and ordained; and this also in the very same sanctuary where he had been before both baptised and ordained.

Irving returned to Newman Street. Here he was met with a message from a prophet speaking in the "power," prohibiting him from the exercise of any priestly function. It is said that he was forbidden even to preach, except in those less sacred assemblies of his Church at which the unbelieving were admitted. Irving himself, it appears, accepted this prophecy with the same unfeigned faith as he had accepted others, and submitted at once to an arrangement which must have gone far to destroy all his authority in his Church.

For some months, apparently, he exercised, with all humility and patience, no higher office than that of a deacon; when at length, by the concurrent action in manifested supernatural power both of prophet and apostle, he was ordained angel, or chief pastor, of the flock assembled in Newman Street. The apostle who acted on this occasion was Mr. Cardale; and from him Irving accepted reordination. Whatever be the views taken of this transaction, we cannot but admire the unfeigned faith of the man who could, in humble obedience, be content to take thus the very lowest room where he had heretofore been chief.

Again, also, was he tried in his own home. A child, named Ebenezer,—no doubt with mystic, and, as he hoped, prophetic, intimation of what he was hereafter to be to his parents,—was taken from them. No divine word of power came on this occasion to rescue the darling from the jaws of death. "The Lord, in His severity and His goodness," Irving said, "had punished him for his sins, and the sin of his flock." Still his faith did not sink; and he went on amidst, as it seems, many difficulties, always springing from the same source—the strange, not to say unsatisfactory, deliverances of the prophetic office. The prophets prophesied in his sanctuary; and their deliverances concerned not things to be hereafter, but chiefly matters of ritual. On these points, the judgment of Irving must have been sorely tried. These external arrangements commanded in the sanctuary were said to be "figures of the true," setting forth mystic meanings and higher truths; but what strikes an observer most, who sees them in the form into which they have now developed, is a similarity to the ritual of that Church which Irving had in other days pronounced "accursed of God—the abomination which His soul hateth." But he ever submitted his private judgment to what he considered the voice of God; and thus his troubled life went on. "The apostles and prophets have patience with him," so writes Mrs. Oliphant in her most touching biography, "when the light breaks slowly through his troubled soul; and, mastering all the prejudices of his life, all the impulses of his will, this martyr, into whose lingering agony nobody enters, still bends his head and obeys."

But his life was not to endure much longer. He had, early in 1834, been sent on a mission to Edinburgh; and here he caught a cold, which threatened disease of the lungs. Having returned from his mission, Mr. Cardale and Mr. Drummond proceeded to Edinburgh, to ordain the Angel of that Church; and continued some time in the North, in order to make other visits, with similar objects. During their absence, a command was given in the "power" to ordain, it appears, certain evangelists—to which command Irving immediately proceeded to give effect. The absent apostles heard of this, and wrote, declaring the new arrangement to be a delusion, and rebuking both prophet and angel. The prophet withdrew for a time in anger; but Irving read the letter in the Church, and confessed his error. Yet there can be no doubt that such difficulties as this circumstance implied did try him sorely. He had looked for a divine, unerring guidance—a really infallible Church; and, behold! that which has a disagreeable likeness to worldly pride and self-conceit. His health, also, was declining; and he, the man who had been so strong and athletic, ailing nothing, now experienced all the lassitude and distress incident to the first stages of that fatal complaint which was consuming him. The prophets, as his disease increased, and alarming symptoms appeared, promised, with more or less of distinctness, that he should be restored; or, at any rate, such was the construction put upon a word spoken in "the power," that he was specially set apart to do a great work in Scotland. He went northwards, the disease increasing all the way, as he slowly journeyed on horseback to his destination. He tried the same remedy as had proved efficacious in the case of cholera, —that is, force of will,—and, wrestling in faith, determined not to give way to the complaint. Consumption was not to be so baffled: it could deceive its victim with what seemed like gleams of returning strength and vigour; but these passed away in their wonted manner, demonstrating to all, except the patient himself, that he rose up weaker from every fresh attack.

On the Menai Bridge, he got wet by the rising of

a sudden squall through the straits. The effect of this was a fevered night; and, though he had strength to ride on to Conway, and thence to Abergele, it was with considerable pain and difficulty. Then, a little recovered again, he at length reached Liverpool. Thence he sent a letter to his wife, asking her to come to him without delay. To her he writes with a presentiment of his coming end, which evidently his faith in the prophets cannot altogether overcome: "Now, my dear, I have sought to serve God, and I do put my trust in Him; therefore I am not afraid. He hath sore chastened me, but He has not given me over to death. I shall yet live, and discover His wonderful works." His wife obeyed the summons, not afraid either; for she, too, put her confidence in that word of "power," which spoke of his being raised up to do a great work. She arrived to find him in a truly alarming state; and, had she possessed eyes to see, it might well have appalled her,—his strength considerably reduced, his pulse 100, and himself looking much worse than when he left home. A southern climate was pronounced by competent medical authority as the only hope, without recourse to which, it was affirmed, he would not survive the winter; but neither husband nor wife could be moved by human appearances, and they went northwards to Greenock, and thence to Glasgow: on arriving at which place, Irving lifted up his hands in thanksgiving, as entering the scene of a great and glorious work. To his friends, it was quite evident that he was sinking rapidly, under a deep consumption. If they pitied his error, they could not but admire his faith, which only breathed trust and confidence in the good purposes of Him who was thus afflicting him; both Irving and his wife being fully persuaded that God, in due time, would renew his strength. Nor did the increase of his sickness open their eyes at all,—a merciful dispensation,—as thus Irving was spared, even to the very last, the terrible mental agony which, had he lived longer, would almost certainly have awaited him, when he found that the sign or the wonder in which he trusted had not come to pass. Nevertheless, as far as failing strength admitted, he still laboured on, nothing of the success promised attending his work. No crowds came to hear him, few were converted; there was no movement towards the Gospel he preached, not even like that which he himself had witnessed before, in this very same place. He was induced, however, apparently as a last hope on the part of his friends, to consult Dr. Stewart; but no aid from man was now possible, and he returned to Glasgow, to the house of the disciple with whom he had taken up his abode. In a few days more, there was no further strength left to him; and he was obliged at last to take to his bed, from which he never arose. The medical attendant who was called in recognised the fatal sign with only too vivid distinctness; and the patient himself admitted that, to all human appearance, the hand of death was upon him. But he never seemed to doubt that he should be raised up, even from beneath the very hand of death itself, to do the work which he believed was appointed for him.

Sometimes his friends had a gleam of hope, as the worst symptoms seemed to relax a little; but these proved to be only the delusive flickerings of the disease—the fever of consumption still raged on. On the Thursday before he died, he began to wander. Up to this point, Mr. Taylor, in whose house he was, believed that he would certainly recover; "his wife," we are told, "never had a doubt of it:" but now even they could deceive themselves no longer. Yet the wanderings of his delirium were such as became his life, and showed that the current of his thoughts was to holy things; they were earnest exhortations, heartfelt prayers. He fancied, moreover, that he was with the weak and suffering of his flock; and made allusions to their special difficulties, which his wife, who knew the circumstances, was partly able to explain. Once he broke out into the strange utterances of what, to the majority of the bystanders, was an unknown tongue. "Jehovah rohi loa ahesar," were the words, which Dr. Martyn, who was near the bed, at once recognised: this time, no broken English sounds, spoken under the influence of excitement; no unknown tongue, which, as a testimony vouchsafed to one who was worthy, was to usher in a new revelation; but yet most truly words of the Spirit, comforting a dying soul. They were the original Hebrew of "The Lord is my Shepherd; I shall not want." And as he went on, speaking more clearly, under the influence of the consoling words, his watcher joined in with the dying man, as he uttered, "Though I walk through the valley of the shadow of death, I will fear no evil; Thy rod and Thy staff they comfort me,"—that ancient oracle, which cheered them both. As he grew more feeble, he seemed as if arguing with himself the question of his own death, which, even in the midst of his delirium, he knew to be drawing near. At length it appeared as though this weighty argument had come to a sufficient conclusion; and the last audible words he uttered were, "If I die, I die unto the Lord. Amen." Then, as the evening of the Lord's Day drew on, he sank to that rest for which he had so ardently longed,—that rest of which he had vainly sought to obtain a glimpse here,—but which nevertheless *remaineth* for the people of God.

He was buried in the crypt of Glasgow Cathedral; and most of the clergy of the city, and a great concourse of devout and earnest men,—who, while they could not but doubt of the soundness of his faith, could not but admire the holiness of the man,—followed him to his grave; and all voices united to proclaim over him, "Blessed are the dead which die in the Lord." If he were deceived, it was his reason, not his heart; if he erred, it was his understanding, not his will. Others might have their spiritual manifestations, and, with a faith largely compounded of self-conceit, might put a blind confidence in their own utterances; but this noble character was of such revelations never found "worthy."

How, it may be asked, did so good a man come to be so deceived, and to propagate his error? The answer is not far to seek. It was another form of that same desire for a visible manifestation, which has done so much mischief in the Church; and, however like faith such an expectation may seem, it is really subversive of all faith, and substitutes something quite different, and even alien from it. It is only a very superficial reading of the New Testament which can induce us to believe that in the early Church itself miraculous gifts were ever more than a sign, altogether occasional in their character. If men had a prophet to whom they might appeal in all cases of difficulty, they need no longer search the Scriptures—they need no longer exercise faith by remaining in a state of anxious expectation; they would then be able, to all intents and purposes, to see. The invisible would become thus, in effect, if not actually, visible, and the veil which now hides it would be taken away. But this is impossible; and the most keen-sighted faith of mortal man never can penetrate the veil,—"No man can see His face, and live:" all that can be hoped for, expected, desired, is the Spirit of God in men's hearts. And this is enough. If there were more than this,—if the Church were *visibly* directed by the external manifestations of an infallible Spirit,—if, by any methods or any gifts, the invisible world could be made so tangible that men could, as it were, with their bodily senses discern it,—then walking by faith would become impossible, men would see with their eyes, and the Apostle's words—his, be it recollected, who saw deepest—could not be applied: "It doth not yet appear what we shall be; but when He shall appear, we shall be like Him, for we shall see Him as He is."

HENRY MARTYN

AND

CHARLES FREDERICK MACKENZIE,

THE MARTYR MISSIONARIES.

Faith loving not Life unto Death.

"For ever with the Lord,—
  Amen, so let it be;
Life from the dead is in that word,—
  'Tis immortality."

MONTGOMERY.

LIVES OF HENRY MARTYN

AND

CHARLES FREDERICK MACKENZIE,

THE MARTYR MISSIONARIES.

HENRY MARTYN was born at Truro, in Cornwall, on February 18th, 1781. His father, John Martyn, was a miner at Gwenap, who, with no more education than such as a country reading-school afforded, nevertheless, by persevering diligence, raised himself from his humble position to be chief clerk in the house of Mr. Daniel, a merchant of Truro, where he enjoyed a tolerable competency.

At the age of seven, Henry was sent to the grammar-school in Truro. Here his talent gave promise of future eminence; nevertheless, he was somewhat idle. His temper, though generally cheerful, was sometimes apt to be peevish and irascible. This no doubt arose partly from feeble health; for he was never very strong. He had not attained his fifteenth year, when he was considered sufficiently advanced to compete for a scholarship at Corpus-Christi College, Oxford. This scholarship he did not obtain, although approaching very closely in merit to the successful candidate. Induced by the desire of being near a valued school-friend, he ultimately entered at Cambridge, and commenced to reside at St. John's College in October 1797. Up to this period, he not only had not displayed any special mathematical talent, but—what, considering the eminence he afterwards attained, is still more remarkable—he even showed a dislike of mathematical investigation. He confesses, also, that he was not as industrious in his first term as he ought to have been: yet he attained to the position of second in the first class of his college examination. At this time, also, though a well-conducted and diligent student, he was not at all religious. His old school-friend, and a sister, were able to exert a salutary influence upon him, and he promised the latter that at Cambridge he would study the Bible; but, as he confesses, Newton engaged all his thoughts.

The sudden death of his father was that which gave the first impulse towards the higher life. Under the impression produced by this great sorrow, he began to read the Bible—at first, because religion was suitable to such a solemn time, and without any vivid interest in, or deep consolation from, it; but after a short time his understanding was opened, and he wrote to his sister, telling her of the change that had come over him, and thus cheering her in the midst of her sorrow with these glad tidings. He soon became a diligent and earnest attendant at Trinity Church, and his acquaintance with Simeon in no small degree tended to his advancement in the knowledge of divine things. It is especially to be observed that, as Martyn grew in grace, so also did he work at his studies more industriously, especially did he give himself up to mathematics, and ultimately obtained the first place in mathematical honours,—or, as it is termed at Cambridge, became senior wrangler. He was elected fellow of St. John's College in March 1802, thus attaining to a position both of usefulness and comfort, and one especially agreeable to one to whom the delights of literary study and intellectual companionship were peculiarly congenial.

But thus early, when the sweets of such a life were in their first delightfulness, he had made up his mind to forsake all for Christ's sake and the Gospel; he determined to become a Christian missionary. The immediate cause of this determination was a remark of Simeon's on the benefit which had resulted from the services of a single missionary in India. But it was not without a strong conflict with himself that he could come to such a resolution. He was a man of deep affections; few could exceed him in love for friends and country. His own health was not strong; and so many of his family were delicate, that to leave them was almost certainly to bid them farewell for ever in this life. He knew that he was forsaking all to follow Christ; and with this purpose in his heart, he offered himself to the Society for Missions to Africa and the East, ready to go whithersoever they might send him.

Yet the real state of his mind, as evidenced in a letter to his sister, was not what some might deem likely as a moving cause for so great a sacrifice. It was not a highly wrought zeal, which surrounded the work he meditated with a halo of glory, concealing the real difficulties and self-denials he would have to encounter. On the contrary, he speaks rather of dejection and despondency,—to one not strong very natural,—and of the recoil from the roughness of such a life. He writes thus: "The dejection I sometimes labour under seems not to arise from doubts of my acceptance with God, though it tends to produce them, nor from desponding views of my own backwardness in the divine life,—for I am more prone to self-dependence and conceit,—but from the prospect of the difficulties I have to encounter in the whole of my future life. The thought that I must be unceasingly employed in the same kind of work, amongst poor, ignorant people, is what my proud spirit revolts at. To be obliged to submit to a thousand uncomfortable things that must happen to me, whether as a minister or missionary, is what flesh cannot endure. At these times, I feel neither love to God nor love to man; and, in proportion as these graces of the spirit languish, my besetting sins—pride and discontent, and unwillingness for every duty—make me miserable."

On Monday, Oct. 22, 1803, Martyn was ordained deacon, and commenced to labour as a minister of the Gospel in Trinity Church, Cambridge, as the curate of Mr. Simeon; undertaking, likewise, the charge of the parish of Lolworth—a small village, at no great distance from the university. The burdens and difficulties of his work lay heavily on his spirit; he even complains that want of private devotional reading, and shortness of prayer, through incessant sermon-making, had produced much strangeness between God and his soul. Yet his ministry was most earnest and diligent—as, indeed, how should it be otherwise?—for he gave himself wholly to the work. His success, however, as a preacher, was not great; his delivery was bad, and there was a defect in his enunciation. He complains, in the course of his journal, how often his preaching met with opposition, especially from amongst the sailors and officers on board the ship in which he sailed to India, and laments this. Yet no one who reads this journal can fail to perceive how thoroughly he is penetrated with the desire to save souls, accompanied with the deepest appreciation of his own unworthiness. But this appears very plainly: he was, perhaps in consequence of his feeble health, desponding; and, self-conscious, he often records the ebb and flow of his religious experiences with a minuteness which is even painful, and which, it appears, did not always conduce to his religious peace. But in this very thing we have another instance of the power of grace, which modifies and subdues the natural disposition by its sanctifying influence, but does not change it in such a sense as would imply another character altogether.

In the early part of the year 1804, Martyn unexpectedly lost his small patrimony; his youngest sister being involved in the same misfortune. This seemed to put an end, for the time, to his missionary aspirations; for he rightly considered that he ought not to leave his sister in distress. The interval of suspense which thus elapsed was employed in the most self-devoted and earnest ministrations in his Cambridge sphere, until the way to the missionary work again opened in an appointment to a chaplaincy under the East-India Company. At this time he visited Cornwall, with the feeling that he should see it and his friends there no more. He had become deeply attached to a young lady in Cornwall: this attachment he did not think he ought to declare; but it gives us some idea of the sacrifice he was making, when we find him writing in his journal thus: "Parted with L—— for ever in this life, with a sort of uncertain pain, which I knew would increase to greater violence." And so it did: his mental agony on the evening of that day, and many succeeding days, was very great; but he was not deterred from his purpose. He bade them all at home farewell, and went forth to the service from which he never returned.

He spent the interval between this visit and the time he actually sailed at Cambridge, absorbed in his pastoral and college duties. Towards the end of January, he received a summons to leave England in ten days; but it was necessary that he should be in priests' orders. This gave him a short respite. He was ordained priest in St. James's Chapel, London, in March; and on April 3d he preached his farewell sermon at Cambridge. The remainder of his time in England was spent in acquiring Hindostanee—a most necessary qualification for one who was to be an Indian missionary. He joined his ship at Portsmouth, which sailed 17th July 1805, in company with a large fleet, under the command of Captain Byng. The fleet put in at Falmouth; and thus Martyn found himself unexpectedly once more amongst his friends. He still, however, held firm in his determination, notwithstanding that he was summoned by an order to sail from the very side of his loved one. He left instantly; and in four hours he was under sail from England. The fleet made little progress during the night; and the next day the coast of Cornwall was still visible. On

Sunday, August 11, with the Mount and St. Hilary's spire still above the horizon, he preached on the text: "But now they desire a better country, that is, an heavenly: wherefore God is not ashamed to be called their God: for He hath prepared for them a city" (Heb. xi. 16). At last, England disappeared; "and with it," he writes, "all my peace. The pains of memory were all I felt. Would I go back? Oh, no! But how can I be supported? My faith fails: I am weak as water." Thus we perceive how great was the sacrifice.

Martyn made efforts to induce those on board to listen to his message of salvation, with no very marked success. The crew, both men and officers, were careless and indifferent; but he comforted himself with the thought that thus he was beginning his missionary work. Yet it is possible that his own very earnestness was something in fault. He could make, and had made, great sacrifices for the truth's sake; yet it may well be, on this very account, that he was unable to enter into the wants of weaker souls: and hence it might have seemed—such could not really have been the fact—that his preaching was deficient in love. We shall see that a brother in the work, who went on the same errand of salvation, won over, by kindliness of manner and personal service, the whole ship's company with which he sailed. Yet he lacked that strong, persistent zeal which Martyn possessed, and was, as he confesses, too much, as Martyn appears to have been too little, influenced by his companions. But the contrast is remarkable: it shows how great is the power of grace.

On his arrival at the Cape, he witnessed a battle. Here, on the field and in the hospital, he was able to speak to the wounded and dying his glorious message. At length, after a voyage which had endured for above nine months, his ship anchored in Madras Roads, at sunrise, April 22d; and on the 14th of May his long and wearisome journey concluded, and he arrived in the country which was to be the scene of his future labours.

Martyn was appointed chaplain at Dinapore. Here he set himself to establish native schools, to attain such a knowledge of Hindostanee as to enable him to preach in that language, and to prepare translations and tracts for dispersion amongst the people. He accordingly devoted himself to this work with all his might; and as Sanscrit forms a kind of parent language to these Oriental tongues, he entered also upon that most difficult of all grammars. He had also his duties as chaplain to the Europeans. At first he was received with almost chilling coldness. Offence was taken at his fervid style of preaching, which was without book; and his flock intimated that they should prefer written compositions. With this request he complied; for, he said, he would give them a folio sermon-book, if they would receive the word of God on that account. We need not wonder, however, that Martyn's plans for the evangelisation of the heathen were coldly received by the Europeans; for if his master, Simeon, was unpopular at home, the disciple could hardly be expected to meet with much better treatment abroad. Nevertheless, his earnestness gathered round him a few souls from among his own people, like-minded with himself. He never appears, however, to have obtained any great success either with the natives or the Europeans. His real talent was that of a linguist and scholar; and in this he found at once his greatest happiness and usefulness. As a translator, he was eminently successful; the occupation was delightful to him. "The time fled so imperceptibly," he says, "while delightfully engaged in translations; the days seem to have passed like a moment."

While deeply occupied in this work, the tidings came to him of the death of his eldest sister. He had already had intimations that her health was failing, so that the blow was thus lightened; yet the affliction to his loving and sensitive nature was very great; but, characteristically, he found in the translation of the Scriptures into Hindostanee at once his distraction and his solace. At this time, also, he was solicited to remove from Calcutta; but the comparative solitude and repose of Dinapore, as compared with a charge in the metropolis of India, induced him to decline the offer, that thus he might have more leisure for his work of translation. He was not disappointed. At this place he completed his version of the New Testament in Hindostanee—only, however, to undertake or superintend others in Arabic and Persian, and to study still more closely the sacred original.

About this time he was removed to Cawnpore, a name since familiar to every European. Here, however, his health began seriously to fail; and it was suggested that he should travel into Arabia and Persia, resting from his ministerial labours, so that thus his strength might be restored, and, at the same time, his knowledge of both Arabic and Persian be improved, and, further, that the versions in these languages—which were deemed not altogether suitable for general distribution—might be rendered more idiomatic and intelligible to the mass of the people. While at Cawnpore, he heard of the death of his youngest sister; so that he was now almost without a relative in the world. Thus, with all that was dear to him gone before, he prepared to take that last journey of his life, which ended in his death amongst strangers, in a strange land.

The journey which he made to Shiraz is an interesting record of new scenes and discussions with the different sects of Mahometans he encountered on his journey. No sooner had he reached Shiraz—the celebrated seat of Persian literature—than he began at once on his work of translation. At Shiraz he continued a year, when at length he pronounced the word "home," and set his face toward England. He was to journey through Constantinople; and then, as it was hoped, having recruited his health in his native country, return again to his labours in India. Not only was the journey wearisome, but Martyn's health became very feeble, and he suffered much from fever. He travelled on, however, to reach Tocat, where the plague was raging; and died either of the fever or the plague,—it is hardly known which,—on the 16th October 1812, in the thirty-second year of his age.

His life is justly regarded as a signal instance of Christian heroism. He gave up literally all for Christ; and, moreover, the sacrifice produced, to all appearance, very trifling immediate results. Other far inferior men than he have apparently done very much more than he was enabled to do for the cause of the Gospel. He did not win many converts; his discussions had no very great influence in leading his Mahometan opponents to a better knowledge; his success as a preacher was but small; his chief works were his translations. Part of the Liturgy, the Parables, and the whole of the New Testament, were translated into Hindostanee, a language intelligible to many millions, from Delhi to Cape Cormorin. By him, or through his means, the Psalms and the New Testament were translated into vernacular Persian. These labours are but the promise of what he might have done, had his life been spared to the service of God's Church. His, then, is a life which is a failure or a success, according to the side on which it is viewed: a failure, regarded from the worldly side,—for but little was accomplished; a success, from the spiritual side,—for few men of modern times have walked more closely with God, or have given themselves up more unreservedly to His service. The Church needs martyrs: she must have continually before her those who are ready to surrender their lives for Christ; and at no time of the Church's history, perhaps, has it been more necessary that this should be set before her than at this present. Missionary effort is wont to be judged by the number of converts made in a given time: a false estimate. What is really needed is a demonstration of the reality and the certainty of the higher life. In these last ages, devotion must play the part that miracle accomplished in the early Church. The martyrdom of St. Stephen was quite as effective towards the spread of the Gospel as the miracle of St. Paul. And so, also, the lives of such men as Martyn and Mackenzie demonstrate, to an age which worships the material and the sensible, the power and presence of the invisible.

Charles Frederick Mackenzie was born at Harcus Cottage, Portmore, Peebleshire, on the 10th of April 1825. He was the youngest of six brothers and five sisters who survived the time of his birth. At five years old, he was left an orphan; and his education devolved to a considerable extent upon his eldest sister. His biography records very little of this godly woman; but her good name, like precious ointment, betrays itself in the course of the history; and we discover that to her judicious training and loving sisterly care was due, under God, that high, earnest spirit which manifests itself in his after life. It is her spirit which lives in her brother, and incites him to deeds of Christian heroism.

On the death of his father, the family removed to Edinburgh; and here the education of Charles was carried on regularly till 1840—first in a private school, then in an academy. As a schoolboy, he was not noted for any particular cleverness, but rather for great conscientiousness and simplicity of character. When quite a child, he had displayed some powers of calculation; and generally he succeeded best in his arithmetic. As he grew older, his mathematical tastes developed. In classics he was never very forward; nor had he much power of learning languages. Nevertheless, when quite a lad, he made some little progress in Hebrew,—probably more with the view of entering holy orders than from any love of the study; for from an early age he had determined to devote himself to the ministry.

His mathematical talent indicated Cambridge as a suitable destination; and in the year 1844 he came into residence as a pensioner of St. John's College. His Scotch origin was at that time an obstacle to his advancement at St. John's College. Restrictions as to birthplace and country, the relics of a very different state of things, existing ages ago, —restrictions which, during the last few years, have altogether been removed,—would have prevented his obtaining a fellowship at St. John's College. He accordingly "migrated" to Caius College. A man who migrates into a college, especially if likely to distinguish himself, is often looked upon with a little jealousy by those already entered as members, because their chance of success is thus diminished by the competition of a stranger; but Mackenzie rapidly became a favourite in his college—as he deserved to be.

At Cambridge, Mackenzie was a sample of the genial and religious reading man. His chief occupation as an undergraduate was, as it ought to have been, his mathematical studies; but he was ready to take part in good works, so far as his time allowed. He accordingly, with the assistance of one of the Cambridge clergy, visited in the Victoria Asylum, — an almshouse for old men and women,—to the inmates of which he used to read the Scriptures. He thus describes his first visit, in a letter to his eldest sister: "I had spent some hours in preparation, before going there, on the two previous days, and on the Sunday itself; but when I got there, though the number was small, in consequence of all that could get to church having gone there for the sacrament, yet I got quite red in the face; and, after reading the chapter (John xiv.), I went over it again, throwing in a few remarks where I could. Then we knelt down, and we read some of the collects and prayers from the Prayer-book. On the whole, I should have felt perfectly miserable, if I had not remembered that, lame and wretched as my endeavour had been, it was better than nothing; for I had read the words of the Bible, and used the prayers of holy men; and that, if I had not gone, *no one else would;* so that I was not stepping in any one's way." This inducement, that *no one else would*, was that which prevailed with him to undertake his missionary work afterwards. It is quite expressive of the character of the man. In his case, it was no overwrought and burning zeal, or, still less, confidence in his own sufficiency, which made him take the lead. If, when the question was proposed, "Whom shall we send, and who shall go for us?" he answered, "Here am I—send me," it was neither rashness nor self-sufficiency which prompted him, but only because other labourers in the Lord's vineyard could not be found.

In January 1848, Mackenzie took his degree. His place was second wrangler. He failed, however, in obtaining that second honour, so prized of Cambridge mathematicians, the Smith's Prize, which was adjudged to the fourth wrangler, Mr. Barry. With this amount of success he was well satisfied; and the more so, as Barry was a personal friend, and the marks were nearly equal. Mackenzie had left Cambridge before the result of this last examination had been declared. He asked a friend to telegraph this result to York, at which place he was to call for the message. The papers of himself and his rival were so nearly of equal merit, that the examiners took additional time to decide; and he received at York this message from his undergraduate friend, who seems to have no doubt that Mackenzie ought to have had the prize: "The muffs have taken time to decide. Keep your tail up!" The telegraph-clerk could not understand the meaning of the strange document; but Mackenzie assured him that it was quite intelligible to him. The account one of his contemporaries gives of him at this time of his life is, "that, though a religious man, and though the groundwork of a true character was discoverable in his childlike simplicity, honesty, and kindness of heart, yet his religion did not at that time shine out with that clearness which was afterwards observable, or apparently influence his life in a marked and predominate manner." On the other hand, his letters to his sister, to whom he writes in all the unreservedness of brotherly affection, show what spirit he was of,—and these discover to us that devotion to the service of God was the chief, the uppermost motive of his soul. Yet the earnestness of his character may well have been somewhat concealed by his very gentleness. Kind-hearted, he would seldom provoke opposition; unassuming, he would keep naturally in the background, if opposition arose. Very likely a more direct religious tone might have been desirable in his words; but his life was eloquent. "It was," says one who knew him intimately, "scarcely possible to be in his society without coming to the conclusion that he had found out the secret of life, and that it would be well to be like him."

After taking his degree, Mackenzie became a fellow of his college; and made up his income, as is usual at Cambridge, by taking private pupils. His destination was, in his own mind, holy orders; and for this he diligently prepared himself. Accordingly, as a layman, he took part in such works of benevolence as were likely to give him an insight into what was to be his future duty. Thus, he undertook the management of a Sunday-school, he was active in the working of the Cambridge Mendicity Society, was secretary of the Cambridge Board of Education, and helped to carry on the Industrial School. He was not very methodical; and his friends used to tell him that, amidst these many occupations, he had the facility of getting into "gigantic messes." Nevertheless, by dint of earnestness and good humour, he generally contrived to extricate himself from these "messes," and made a most efficient fellow-helper, seldom failing to accomplish somehow what he had promised to do. At the same time, he was diligent in those special studies which should engage one who was preparing for the ministry,—especially, it appears, Hebrew and the Greek Testament. His life at Cambridge was, like so many useful lives, uneventful. He took considerable pains to obtain an influence over the undergraduates: he was a diligent college lecturer, a careful private tutor, a good oar in the college boat, and a good bat in the cricket-field. And the example of this simple life—of one who joined in the sports of his juniors, a mentor but little older than themselves, kind and genial, as well as religious —displayed and communicated good to all around. In the year 1851, he was ordained deacon at the Trinity-Sunday ordination by the Bishop of Ely. No great and marked change was made in his life by this event, save only that as, when a lay fellow of his college, he had endeavoured to set an example to his lay brethren, so now, as a clergyman, did he purpose that his college should be, for the present, his parish, and that he would especially seek to do God's work in it. He soon, however, felt a desire for more direct ministerial employment; and, on an assistant-curacy offering at Haslingfield, a village near Cambridge,—and which yet did not take him away from his college-work,—he accepted the offer; and used to walk five and a half miles out and home every Sunday, finding, as might be expected, college and parish work combined very heavy indeed. He says, in a letter to his sister: "I have been reading Evans's *Bishopric of Souls.* He has given me a great longing for a country parish, and nothing else to do; but I believe I am more useful as I am." The parish-work was accompanied with a great deal of university-work. Mackenzie was successively Examiner, and then twice Moderator, in the great mathematical examination of Cambridge. To fulfil these important offices is a high honour, but also a heavy charge. The preparation of the questions for this examination is only intrusted to men of high mathematical standing, and requires much pains and a long preparation. The senior Moderator, as he is called at Cambridge, is the head of a board of examiners, consisting of four persons; and on him, above his colleagues, devolve special responsibilities in conducting an examination which endures for a week, and at which considerably over a hundred of the most diligent students are examined. Even Mackenzie, with his love of being useful, and his elastic spirit, was almost appalled by such a work. He writes to his sister, almost four months before the examination: "Then I never forget that I have problems to make for January;" and he complains to her that his parish has suffered in consequence. On the 19th of September 1852, he was ordained priest. No special reference is found in his letters to this event. A probable reason of this silence is that, as he went home almost immediately afterwards, he communicated with his beloved sister, face to face, his aspirations, hopes, and fears.

In 1853, his duties as Moderator took up so much time, that he wisely obtained help for his parish; and the Rev. W. Hutt, of Caius College, undertook his duties, and, on his leaving England, became his successor. Soon after his examination-work was completed, his thoughts began to turn to that mission-field in which he was to make his fame and lose his life. The immediate occasion of this was the Delhi mission. The Rev. J. S. Jackson, also a member of Caius College, and three years his junior, was the first missionary. Jackson came to his own college in hopes to find there, if possible, one who would go out with him as a fellow-helper; and the example of his devotion caused Mackenzie to reflect whether he too might not offer himself. He discusses the point in a letter to his sister, describing how he "broached the matter to Jackson, and found him not indisposed to have himself as a companion." He observes, that many were ready to say to him, "'I wish I could find some one else to go with you,' but did not offer to go themselves." Mackenzie also considered that he ought hardly to say to the young men, "'You had better go out to India,' when he was hugging himself in his comfortable place at home." Considering, then, the scarcity of labourers for this field of harvest, he writes, in conclusion: "I took a long walk, and thought it well over; and made up my mind that God would approve of the change, that Christ would approve, that the Holy Spirit would help me in it. I thought my dear mother would have smiled through her tears at the plan, if she had still lived; and that she would now rejoice without grief. I thought you would give me your solid and sober judgment upon it, and I thought your judgment would be in favour." And then, after some other points relative to his successor at Caius, and the way in which means might be provided for the work, and other topics, he adds, as reasons against the plan: "I freely confess I can see nothing against it except my own unfitness. I am rather afraid of my own instability and want of method and perseverance, habits which have been increasing with me of late. I am rather afraid of their injuring the cause I am going to undertake." Now, surely nothing can be more in accordance with true Christian humility than this letter, intended, be it observed, for no other eyes than those of the sister to whom it is addressed; for he bids her keep his counsel. He is ready to go as the second to a man three years his junior, and sees no objection but his own unfitness. He is ready, moreover, to offer himself, because others, whom he thinks more worthy, would not volunteer. On this occasion, however, the result was that he did not go to India. His friends were averse to the plan, not because they thought him unfit, but because they considered that he was so useful in his college life and work that he could not well be spared. Another was ultimately found who went out in the place which he had wished to occupy, and who died a martyr; for he was murdered at Delhi during the Indian mutiny. Mackenzie returned to his useful, unobtrusive employments at the university; but he did not give up the idea of missionary work, when he should be more easily spared, and a more suitable post be found for him.

November 30, St. Andrew's Day, 1853, proved in more ways than one to be a memorable day in the history of the Church of England. On that day were consecrated, in the parish-church at Lambeth, the first Bishops of Graham's Town and Natal. The Bishops of Cape Town and New Zealand had just returned to England, and both set forth the claims of their vast dioceses. The latter especially received a warm response in Cambridge, his own university; and his eloquent and heart-stirring addresses, as well as his noble example, moved many hearts to help in the great work. Bishop Colenso went out to Natal, and, after a short sojourn there of ten weeks, returned, in order to collect funds, and make arrangements for the extension of the mission-work in that diocese. The Bishop of Natal—himself a member of St. John's College, and who had obtained in his day the same high mathematical honours as Mackenzie possessed—proposed to the latter to go out with him as archdeacon. This offer Mackenzie at first declined, apparently in deference to the wishes of his family; but, having heard Bishop Selwyn's discourses in the university pulpit, setting forth the great need there was of men ready to undertake the work of evangelisation in the colonies, he reconsidered his determination, and accepted the offer. It was an act of self-sacrifice. If he had thought of mere worldly advancement, his high position at the university, had he elected to remain there, would probably have led to all he could desire. But none of these things moved him; neither counted he his life dear unto himself, that he for Christ's sake might preach the Gospel of the grace of God, and that not with any high-flown zeal and enthusiasm, or any feeling of self-sufficiency, as though he would do the work better than others, but simply because labourers were needed for the harvest, and no one else seemed ready to go.

On May 7th, 1855, the missionary party sailed, and met with little adventure, except that we find the Venerable Archdeacon, who, though sea-sick himself, has fortunately no headache, waiting upon the steerage-passengers, who, very sea-sick, had both heartache and headache. For these he makes arrowroot, and to these administers brandy and raspberry-vinegar, and other little comforts, very refreshing to sea-sick passengers; and by this means establishes—and no wonder—a very friendly feeling between the different parts of the ship. There was on board a daily service, morning and evening; this, with reading the Scriptures, and working at the Zulu language, formed the day's operations—very uneventful, almost commonplace, and yet how truly apostolic and useful! On May 20th, they were in sight of land; and, after a most prosperous and happy passage of seventy days, the missionary party landed in the colony. His sister, who took part in his noble work, writing home an account of her brother, thus describes him: "He is the life of the party, the sunshine of the steerage, and the director of every thing, from the boxes in the hold to the preaching and teaching of all on board."

Mackenzie had come out with the idea of being a missionary. It was judged, however, desirable that he should, at any rate for the present, settle down as the parish-priest of the colonial town of Durban; which, though against his own feeling and judgment, he did in deference to the wishes of his ecclesiastical superiors. It seemed to his friends almost like a waste of power to take him from the general missionary work of the colony, and set him down as the mere parish-priest of an inconsiderable white population. His ministrations at Durban were apparently the least useful and successful of any. It was the bishop's wish to introduce the offertory, and also the surplice for preaching; though he did not authoritatively enjoin these observances. Mackenzie, on mentioning to one of the churchwardens what was proposed, received as a reply: "You do not know what a storm you will raise. I, for my part, cannot collect the offertory in defiance of the feelings of the people." Of course, the usual results followed; the soul of this good, kind man was vexed with a squabble —for, after all, it was nothing better—about a mere matter of ecclesiastical routine; and concession on Mackenzie's part, peacemaker though he were, failed to soothe the rancour of the controversy. His ministry in Durban continued a year and a half, during which time his life was embittered by the dissensions created, and the troubles connected with them. It is but just, however, to both parties to say that, on Mackenzie's return to Durban at a subsequent period, he was welcomed by all with the heartiness due to his simple and truly liberal-minded Christianity.

In 1857, Mackenzie entered on another sphere of work; this was the district of Umhlali. Here he was joined by another sister, Miss Alice Mackenzie, who was a great addition to the strength of the party; with great zeal and considerable success giving herself up to the missionary work amongst the natives. He used playfully to call her, from the interest she took in the native race, his "black sister." Their life here was both happy and useful. They were, indeed, far away from European luxuries, and fared, considering that they had been used to all the appliances and comforts of an English home, somewhat hardly. But these were only light self-denials.

Mackenzie himself worked with apostolic diligence. A sketch of a Sunday's occupation, communicated in a letter by his sister, will illustrate this. She writes: "His Sunday labours are very intense. He has short, early Kaffir prayers, then breakfast at half-past seven, full service at the camp for the soldiers at nine—it is about two miles off. As soon as he comes back, the congregation is assembling here, and his horse is saddled for him to mount as soon as the service is over. He has another service at Mount Moreland, about sixteen miles off, at three p.m. In coming here, he showed us the spot where his horse always knows that he may walk instead of trotting, to allow him to eat his dinner of sandwiches. The ride in the sun is very knocking up both for him and his horse. He told us he was in similar circumstances to Elijah, as the brook he used to drink from is now dried up. His horse is again ready for him when this service is over, and he rides to Verulam—either four or six miles, I forget which—where he has service at six p.m. in Mr. ——'s house. He goes to sup with a kind Dutch lady, and spends the night with Mr. ——. . . . He tells us that he may not always return home till Tuesday, but do parish-visiting work at that end of his parish." A very tolerable Sunday's work, surely; and this was relieved on week-days with schools for the children, both white and black, and popular lectures to the soldiers. The ladies of the family were as diligent as their brother, and loved their work. "Is not this," writes a sister, "a happy life?" Truly, for it is more blessed to give than to receive. And, in this continual round of Christian usefulness, the days and weeks passed rapidly away.

Yet even this happy time was not without its trials. His eldest sister was in failing health, and not expected to live; and the February mail, 1859, brought the intelligence of her death. But though the missionary family sorrowed, it was with a chastened grief. They felt the parting was a short one; as, indeed, in Mackenzie's own case, it proved to be but very short. And so they lived on in undiminished faith and patience, and in increasing usefulness.

Notwithstanding Mackenzie's great and incessant labours, he was never seriously ill. Once, indeed, a sunstroke seemed to threaten; but timely rest recovered him in a few hours, and the weakness subsided in a week or two, leaving him able, at the end of the time, to continue his work as before.

In April, rather unexpectedly, it was arranged that he should return to England; and accordingly he arrived in July 1859.

England had just been startled and delighted with an account of the wonderful discovery of Livingstone, resulting in the solution of that long-sought mystery, the sources of the Nile. But Livingstone was a missionary; and he desired to make his discovery subordinate to the great cause he had at heart, the evangelisation of the country he had so wonderfully opened up. Himself a Scotchman and a Presbyterian, he was liberal enough to rise superior to all narrow provincial or sectarian jealousy, and determined to appeal for help to the Universities of Oxford and Cambridge.

On December the 4th, 1857, Dr. Livingstone appeared in the Senate-House at Cambridge, for the purpose of giving a lecture on his travels; Dr. Philpott, then Vice-chancellor and Master of St. Catherine's College, now Bishop of Worcester, in the chair. The reception was enthusiastic. The concluding words of the lecturer were: "I go back to Africa to try to make an open path for commerce and Christianity. Do you carry out the work I have begun; I leave it with you." The idea which resulted was a happy one: it was to plant a mission in Central Africa, and so dry up the slave-trade at its source, by the combined influences of Christianity and the development of legitimate trade. A society was formed in Cambridge to carry this idea into practice. The coöperation of the sister university was sought, and most heartily given; and so was commenced "The Oxford-and-Cambridge Mission to Central Africa." In 1858, the Bishop of Cape Town arrived in England, with somewhat similar objects,—to find, however, that the mission-scheme had already taken shape; and then, unexpectedly, Mackenzie appeared upon the scene, his own intention being simply to pay a short visit in

England, and either go to the Zulu country, or back to Natal, as might afterwards be arranged.

We may turn aside here for a moment to observe, that Mackenzie showed the same kind-hearted attention on the return voyage as on the way out. The steamer *Waldensian*, in which he journeyed, was crowded, and the weather rough. An American missionary, and his wife and six children, were all ill; Mackenzie waited on them, and dressed the little ones. The troubles of another family were further intensified by the confinement of the mother. When her hour came, she said no one could be of any comfort except the archdeacon; he went at once to her bedside, prayed with her, and then went to superintend the getting her boxes out of the hold. A few days after, he baptised the infant by the name of Charles Frederick Mackenzie, at the special request of the parents; himself and sister acting as sponsors.

Mackenzie was requested to become head of the new mission, and he accepted the office at once; but he knew what acceptance of the offer involved—it was nothing less than the probable sacrifice of his own life. It is also to be observed that, at the time when the proposal was made, the question whether the head of the mission should be a bishop or not had not been decided, so that he was not moved by prospects of ecclesiastical advancement,—though, if he had been, it would have been a noble ambition,—for that any presbyter should desire the higher office, is indeed to desire a "good work;" and, in this particular instance, surely the good work had very few extraneous recommendations. It was, however, at length decided that he should be consecrated bishop; but, in consequence of certain legal considerations, this consecration was arranged to take place in Cape Town: whither he proceeded, in company with Rev. J. L. Procter; Rev. H. C. Scudamore; Mr. Horace Waller, lay superintendent; S. A. Gamble, a carpenter; and Alfred Adams, an agricultural labourer. The sister who accompanied him on his first voyage was also his companion on this occasion. The *Cambrian* steamer carried the party; and, after an uneventful voyage, they arrived at the Cape on Nov. 12. Here they were enthusiastically received, and preparations were made for the consecration of the bishop.

The service on which the missionary party were entering was one of difficulty and danger; not the least danger is the deadly fever which lurks every where on the coast of Africa, and which forms a formidable barrier to intercourse with that great country. While at the Cape, news came that the members of the Makololo mission, under the London Missionary Society, had already fallen victims to fever. But these dangers did not deter Mackenzie and his fellows. Alluding to what he calls most truly "the sad destruction of life, and the loss of

Christian energy and zeal, in the person of those who have lately been cut off in the interior of the country," he says: "It has been said that we who are going up are not to be daunted by that. No; rather it should be the opposite—rather should we go up now with a more firm determination and intention, God helping us, of carrying on the work. . . . It may be that, in the course of years, we may become, what I have sometimes thought we were, like the original and early sprouts which rise from the seed in the ground, and which serve but to give life and vigour and energy to the shoots which rise above the ground afterwards:" words which indeed proved prophetic; but these were men who took their lives in their hands for the sake of the Gospel, and *lost* them,—but that loss is greatest gain.

The consecration of Mackenzie as missionary bishop took place in the cathedral of Cape Town: and thus went to his labours the first missionary bishop sent out by the Church of England. Mackenzie regarded this as most important. "I am very thankful," he says, "that all has ended as we hoped. I have said several times, that if I was to go at the head of this mission, as it was in any case the work of a bishop, I ought not to be sent without the authority, and, still more, the grace of God given in consecration. Besides this, I feel strongly that it is the right course; and that, whether there be any marked success in this mission or not, on the whole we may hope for more rapid, sound, and united progress."

It was highly desirable that, if possible, interpreters should be found for the party, as the languages amongst which they were going were quite strange to them all. These were found in a coloured congregation at Cape Town, under the charge of an English clergyman, Mr. Lightfoot. The congregation consisted of liberated slaves—persons who had been captured by British cruisers from slave-vessels on the east coast of Africa, and liberated at Cape Town. Intercourse amongst themselves kept up their own language; while many had acquired the English tongue by long residence in the colony. Mackenzie preached to these black people one Sunday, and asked who would volunteer to go with him on his errand of mercy to their brethren. Not less than twelve stood up; and several went with the party, and proved of incalculable service to the mission. So was the slave-trade the means by which the providence of God worked to bring the knowledge of the Gospel to those poor heathen who groaned under its tyrannies.

These arrangements made, Mackenzie and his party sailed for the Shirè River, on the banks of which it was proposed that he should settle. What the bishop's own visions of episcopal responsibilities were, can be gathered from a conversation with his sister as he parted with her. She was speaking of happiness; he said: "I have given up looking for that altogether. Now till death my post is one of unrest and care. To be the sharer of every one's sorrows, the comforter of every one's griefs, the strengthener of every one's weakness,—to do this as much as in me lies, is now my aim and object; for you know, when the members suffer, the pain must always fly to the head."

The voyage up the river was tedious and laborious; and here the missionaries first became acquainted with their deadliest enemy—that is, the African fever. The earlier attacks of the fever were slight. This proved unfortunate, as thereby they were all too much disposed to underrate the danger incurred. The details of this voyage, which has all the interest of an exploring-party, cannot be given here; they will be found at length in the beautiful memoir by Dean Goodwin. It may suffice to observe that Mackenzie showed the same indefatigable good humour and patient endurance as ever. The bishop's hands, on one occasion, were sore with the labour of hauling the vessel off the sand-banks; he, too, was always ready for a spell at cutting the wood used for fuel under the boilers. His great desire, however, all through this long journey, was to get as speedily as possible to the scene of his labours; and this appears in all his letters: above all, there is continually before him the higher and better life. Just as he nears the ground, at the end of his laborious river-voyage, he writes to a friend: "And if we shall not soon, perhaps in some cases never, meet our old friends on earth, we have a sure and certain hope of a better meeting. It is pleasant to look forward to the one; it is life and joy to be sure of the other."

On arriving at a point on the river Shirè called Chibisas, on July 8, the missionary party left the steamer, and proceeded on foot in search of a settlement. The object was to find some high land, on which they would be more free from fever. The people amongst whom they were located are known as Mang-anja; they are a weak race, as compared with their neighbours, the Ajawa. The whole district is a slave-hunting and slave-dealing territory, and the weaker races suffer most, but are themselves by no means indisposed, when the opportunity occurs, to engage in the horrible traffic. Thus the question at once arose as to the position the missionaries ought to take in the quarrels and raids of these slave-hunters. Could they try non-intervention, and determine under no circumstances to use their guns, except in self-defence? This strongly recommended itself as the right course to Mackenzie. Unfortunately, he was unable to follow it; he was involved in one of these quarrels even before he had encamped upon the ground he had chosen for his settlement. And once, however reluctantly, having taken part in a native quarrel, to withdraw would have subjected him to a charge of either cowardice or indifference, or both.

The missionaries were on their way to the station; Mackenzie was sitting on a package, in the middle of a village, with a companion, reading the Psalms of the day, and chanting the doxologies, partly because fond of music, partly that the natives might thus perceive the errand on which their visitors had come. On the Psalms being ended, Mackenzie, Procter, and Scudamore went down to the stream to bathe. They heard the sound of penny trumpets, and fancied that Livingstone had been giving away presents. It appeared, however, that these trumpets, notwithstanding their ignominious character, had a most serious meaning. A party of six men had entered the village with eighty-four slaves. The men, finding the English in the village, had run away; the slaves were free. All the English guns were out, though these conscience-stricken wretches had needed no firing to hasten their flight. The firing-party acted, it is to be observed, under the direction of Dr. Livingstone; so that, whatever be thought of the policy of the affair, Mackenzie was in no way responsible for it. In this way a large body of liberated captives were suddenly placed at the disposal of the missionaries, who could hardly do otherwise than take charge of them. But the consequences of this event were very serious. The missionaries had come to preach the Gospel, but thus early in their career did they stand before the country as slave-liberators. They can hardly be said to have taken the sword,—it was thrust into their hands; but thus, nevertheless, they were placed before the eyes of the natives in a very different position from that which, as mere preachers and teachers, they had proposed to themselves. They had now, as it were, a tribe of their own. The bishop had become an African chief, and he could settle down, not as a visitor, but as the head of a population, the father of a family; and not only must teach, but, if need be, protect, his children.

The missionaries had to choose a station, and a place called Magomero was selected. Its chief advantage was, that it was included by a sharp bend of the river in such a manner that, by running a stockade across from bank to bank, the included land could be rendered safe from attack. On the other hand, the place was low, and covered with wood, and was thus unhealthy; so that, in the rainy season especially, there was much fever. It was also no less than sixty miles distant from the river Shirè, which formed the high-road by which the missionary party were connected with the civilised world. It is very possible that a better site, had all the circumstances been foreseen, would have been chosen; but the position in which Mackenzie found himself had not been anticipated by any one.

The first consideration was the erection of huts for residences, and at this the bishop laboured with his usual diligence; at the same time, a beginning was made in the instruction of the children, by drilling and school-exercise, until a better communication should be established, when the language had been learned. The life of the missionaries was peaceful and happy; and, had it not been for the wars which were being waged around them, and in which, unfortunately, they became involved, they might possibly have become *at once* a fountain of Gospel truth in the moral wilderness.

But the Ajawa were devastating the country, and their Mang-anja friends again applied to Mackenzie and his party for assistance. This Mackenzie was induced to give, partly because he considered that he was engaging in what was simply a war of self-defence, and protection of the captives under his care, so many of them being orphans; and partly because he hoped to be able to obtain a law from the Mang-anja, prohibiting altogether the slave-trade for the future. To this law his allies readily agreed. The English accordingly went against the enemy, who were easily subdued; the result being still further to increase the little colony under the direction of the bishop. There seemed also to be another advantage attending this circumstance,—that thus the missionaries should at once set forth the Gospel in its practical form of a defence for the weak and oppressed, until such time as an increasing knowledge of the language should enable them to expound its special doctrines more perfectly. That this was a mistake, the event has proved; such a policy, to be carried out successfully, would have required that Mackenzie should combine the powers of a general with the authority of a bishop. The mission-station should have been chosen so as at once to have been healthy, in order that the strength of the party might be fully preserved; and strong, so as to be able to resist for a considerable time any force the natives were likely to be able to bring against it. Even then the policy of the leader ought to have been strictly defensive; at any rate, until such time as the consolidation of his power and influence, and his acquaintance with the country, should have enabled him to interfere with effect on whichever side he considered to be just and right. It turned out, in the event, that the invasion of the Ajawa was not the onslaught of a mere slave-taking raid, but a steady invasion by a stronger race upon a weaker; and it was not only impolitic and dangerous to incur their animosity, but it was of the greatest importance to win such a race over to the Gospel: but of this circumstance the missionaries did not become aware till after the death of Mackenzie. Then, again, the presence of a native population in a settlement at best unhealthy was an additional source of disease to the Europeans, who found it most difficult to enforce any thing like a sanitary police. After all, fever was the ever-present and deadly enemy of the Europeans. It was to this enemy that not only Mackenzie succumbed, but several of the leaders of the mission as well.

Nevertheless, apart from premonitory attacks, showing that this enemy ought not to have been despised, matters proceeded so far favourably, that Mackenzie deemed it prudent to send for the ladies of the party. The missionaries had already received a considerable addition in the person of the Rev. H. De Wint Burrup; Mr. Dickinson, M.D., the medical officer of the expedition; and Thomas Clarke, a tanner. This party had pushed up rapidly from the sea to Magomero, defying all the usual precautions against fever, and, as it happened, with success; for they all arrived in good health at Magomero. This, of course, made them think lightly of African fever. Mrs. Burrup had come out with her husband, but remained behind with Miss Mackenzie, to join the party when the settlement should be sufficiently established to make their reception a matter of prudence. This time, Mackenzie judged, had now arrived; and arrangements were made that he and Mr. Burrup should go and meet them at a small island, at the point where the Ruo and Shirè meet. Accordingly, Dr. Livingstone was to bring the ladies to this point, at which it was expected they would arrive about the beginning of January. But delays occurred, and Mackenzie did not arrive at the place of meeting until the 13th of January. Livingstone had passed a few days before on his way down. It so happened that the medicines had been lost by an accidental upsetting of the canoe in which Mackenzie journeyed down the river. The bishop, who seemed from former experience to be comparatively fever-proof, greatly underrated the danger of remaining in this place; and thus, though on an island near a marsh, without quinine, and in a state of inaction after strong labour,—in circumstances, that is, rendering him especially liable to an attack of fever,—he determined to stay at a spot which must necessarily have been, even under the most favourable circumstances, unhealthy. Mackenzie was further induced to take this step by a favourable opportunity, as it seemed to him, of making friends with the chief, and so laying the foundation for future missionary work; but here, in the midst of his plans for the evangelisation of the natives, the fever seized upon him, and made rapid progress. He became aware that his end was drawing near, and told his native attendants that Jesus was coming to fetch him away. About the 20th of January, his senses began to fail, and he lay in his hut in extreme weakness; on the 24th, he appears to have ruptured a blood-vessel. Mr. Burrup, his companion, was nearly as ill as himself, and could thus render but little assistance. His native attendants did all they could, being faithful and attentive to the last. On the morning of the 31st, the chief insisted that the bishop should be removed to another hut; the probable motive being, that he feared lest the bishop's death should take place in his hut, and thus, according to their superstition, the hut would be haunted by his spirit. Mr. Burrup was obliged to consent, for fear of worse consequences; and the dying bishop was removed to the other hut. This probably hastened his end, as in about an hour and a half afterwards he breathed his last.

Mr. Burrup, ill as he was, had at once to take steps for the removal of the body, which the chief insisted should not remain where it was even for a day; on the same evening, therefore, assisted by the faithful natives, the body was conveyed in a canoe to the mainland, and there, in a secluded spot, under a large tree, a grave was dug, and, as the evening darkened around him, Mr. Burrup, himself a dying man, committed the body of his brother to the dust.

Mr. Burrup immediately made preparations for a return to Magomero, leaving a letter for Dr. Livingstone and the ladies with the chief. He arrived there on February 14th, so exhausted with fever as to be unable to walk. It was hoped he might, by care and medicine, yet survive; but he sunk on February 22d, and was buried in a quiet spot on the following day, which was Sunday, near Magomero.

The ladies of the party had arrived, and reached in due time the place of rendezvous; Miss Mackenzie, at that time, being unconscious from fever. Inquiry was made concerning the bishop; but the natives denied all knowledge of him, although the letter was in their hands,—fearing they might be called to account for the bishop's death. This caused a harassing suspense, which endured till March 4, when the real facts were ascertained. Nothing now remained but that the sorrowing party should return to the Cape, at which place they arrived safely on April 26.

Thus, then, was consummated this noble act of self-sacrifice and Christian heroism, in which two noble-minded men had sacrificed their lives, and two Christian heroines surrendered what was dearest to them on earth: and willingly surrendered; for all, knowing the risk, deliberately hazarded their lives for the sake of the Gospel. It may be said, indeed, on cold, calculating worldly principles, that such lives are lost; but so only, by men who love not their lives unto the death, can THAT kingdom be advanced.

It is interesting to compare the two lives of the Martyr Missionaries, who stand side by side in this little book; both are so wonderfully alike, and yet so marvellously different. To a superficial observer, they may be supposed to have belonged to altogether different schools of religious thought: Mackenzie the modern High Churchman, who introduces the surplice and the offertory; Martyn the Evangelical, who only preaches from book because his people wish it. And then, also, their dispositions were as different as their ecclesiastical leanings: Mackenzie, robust and cheerful, is always ready for active bodily service; Martyn, feeble and desponding, is soon exhausted. Mackenzie is impressible, easily, even too easily, influenced by those with whom he happens to be; Martyn is one who, in spite of a certain softness, can stand alone in decided, though conscientious, antagonism to those to whom he is opposed. Mackenzie attracts all by a kind of instinct, and is almost idolised by those over whom he rules; Martyn makes but few friends, and seems almost to repel those for whom he nevertheless burns with Christian love and zeal. The talent of the one is displayed in the active life of the missionary bishop; of the other, in the pains and skill by which he renders the truth of the Holy Word intelligible to his converts. Yet, notwithstanding all these great differences, how wonderfully similar is the life of both! The history of the one, in the most important of all particulars, is the history of the other. Under the influence of grace, they both give themselves wholly to the work; for this they both leave their university, with its pleasant, useful life, though appreciating its pleasantness, and aware of its usefulness. They forsake home friends, all that is near and dear, impelled by one motive, "that they might finish their course with joy, and the ministry they had received, to testify the Gospel of the grace of God."

The value, then, of such lives as are set forth in these two contrasted biographies, is not at all to be measured by the success which attended the labours of their earthly existence. They set forth, indeed, even more strongly than those other lives here recorded, that which it was especially our purpose to demonstrate,—the power of the invisible; for, just as the most touching memorial of bravery and patriotism is not found in the marble monument of the general in the aisle of the cathedral, but in the nameless graves of rank and file which dot the surface of the battle-field, so is it with the soldiers of the cross. There is a marvellous tale of Christian heroism in that solitary grave amidst the reeds of the Shirè, and the unknown sepulchre in the burial-place at Tocat. If regarded from the world's point of view, there is no work, nor device, nor knowledge, nor wisdom, in these humble graves; yet, from the Christian side, they speak with an eloquence which strikingly displays the power of godliness over men's hearts, and the strength with which the invisible prevails. It is in such biographies as these that our age, which delights so much in what it calls material results, may find what is to it a needful evidence of Christianity—the evidence afforded by the power which the Gospel displays to bend to its ministry men of sound judgment and cultivated taste. These men of whom we write were not mere enthusiasts; on the contrary, both of them had had that kind of education which would, even if they had been previously inclined that way, have purged out enthusiasm from them. They were both accomplished mathematicians, with minds drilled by the inflexible reasonings of that most matter-of-fact of all studies. Yet these men, at the call of what they held to be their duty to an inferior and despised race, took their lives in their hands, and, in the calmest and most deliberate manner possible, sacrificed every thing they had, in order to accomplish their ministry—a sure proof that they had a demonstration of the existence of the unseen as cogent as, even more so than, that which mathematics supplied in the visible. And this demonstration was no other than that which prevails with Christians, and always will,—the demonstration of the Spirit.

There is also another point which, in conclusion, we would especially desire to remark on; and this is, the analogy which exists between the propagation of Christianity and its original foundation. It must never be forgotten that Christianity was established by the death of its Founder. We need not marvel, therefore, that its progress should be analogous with its commencement, and that martyrdoms and sacrifices should promote its ultimate victory as much as, even more than, the open and immediate success of its ministers. Thus regarded, it will be seen that these lives were sacrificed not without result. That an age of engrossing worldliness, which absolutely worships success, should have from time to time set before it the example of those who, in opposition to the tendency of their times, are ready to give their lives for that old faith which supercilious unbelief pronounces to be almost effete, is a wholesome reminder that the unseen is not so distant and evanescent as they who have no hopes for it, or aspirations after it, would gladly believe it to be.

AN EPILOGUE OF CONTRASTS.

I.

Ah, how vainly, ah, how quickly,
  Mortal life is passing!
Like a vapour, changing ever,
Shifting, fleeting, stable never,
Then in darkness quenched for ever.

II.

Ah, how stable, ah, how joyful,
  Life on Christ depending!
Free from trouble, safe for ever,
It abideth, changing never,
Hid with Christ in God for ever.

III.

Ah, how fleeting, disappointing,
  Earthly love appeareth!
Hearts which cling most close together,
Partings sad must often sever;
And, at last, "farewell for ever!"

IV.

How surpassing, satisfying,
  Love in Jesus grounded!
Its length and breadth and depth whoever
Comprehends, the height can measure,
Of love which passeth knowledge ever?

V.

Art thou knowing or devising
  But man's works and wisdom?
See, then, thou art going thither,
Where they all will end together,
Silent in the grave for ever.

VI.

Art thou working, art thou dying,
  In the faith of Jesus?
Then thy works shall follow whither
Thou, in blessed rest and pleasure,
Shalt live and reign with Christ for ever.

VII.

Quickly fading, not abiding,
  Is the worldling's glory!
Like the chaff and dust together
Blown before the angry weather,
Scattered by the wind for ever.

VIII.

How enduring and how lasting
  Is the Christian's blessing!
Like the tree which, blowing ever
By life's crystal, shining river,
Is rooted in God's love for ever.

Imitated from the German.

LONDON:
LEVEY AND CO., PRINTERS, GREAT NEW STREET,
FETTER LANE, E.C.

Captain Penny, the Veteran Whaler.

ADVENTURES in the ICE: a Comprehensive Summary of Arctic Exploration, Discovery, and Adventure, including Experiences of Captain Penny, the Veteran Whaler, now first published. With Portraits of Sir John Franklin, Captain Penny, Dr. Elisha Kent Kane, Dr. Isaac I. Hayes, and Fourteen other Illustrations. By JOHN TILLOTSON. Price 3*s.* 6*d.*

Edinburgh Courant.—"We could scarcely imagine a better or more enjoyable book for boys than this. It consists of stories, adventures, and illustrations—with this advantage, that the stories are all true, the adventures actually took place, and the illustrations are all from real life. . . . It will almost infallibly chain the attention."

Birkenhead Advertiser.—"Well written, and illustrated with many good engravings; while its price brings it within the reach of all. Mr. Tillotson has been indebted to the kindness of Captain Penny for an amount of information as to the whale-fishery which is most interesting."

Athenæum.—"A fairly written and concise summary, . . . containing a stirring account of the several voyages of Captain Penny, and of his adventures with shoals of whales."

The World's Progress.

PIONEERS of CIVILISATION. By the Author of "Lives of Eminent Men," &c.

The Soldier-Pioneer.
Pioneers of Enterprise and Daring.
Exploring Pioneers.
Peaceful Pioneers.
Trading Pioneers.
Settling Pioneers.
The Pioneers of Faith.

With Portraits of Dr. Livingstone, Captain Clapperton, William Penn, Captain Cook, Lord Robert Clive, Captain Flinders, Rev. Henry Martyn, and Eight other Page Illustrations. Price 3*s.* 6*d.*

Art Journal.—"This is a most agreeable book, well and sensibly written."

Literary World.—"We like both the title and the plan of this book. . . . It would be difficult to find a book more calculated to interest and benefit an intelligent youth."

Freeman.—"The style is graphic, the tone manly and good. The book is sure to become a favourite."

Daily Telegraph.—"It is a good little book."

Fun.—"In *Pioneers of Civilisation,* Messrs. Hogg follow up their book of Arctic exploration, and continue a series which will delight our boys, and even the 'boys of larger growth.'"

The Christian Life of the Present Day.

THE PATH on EARTH to the GATE of HEAVEN: Essays of Counsel and Encouragement for the Christian Life of the Present Day. By the Rev. FREDERICK ARNOLD, of Christ Church, Oxford. New and Cheaper Edition. With a Frontispiece. Price 3*s.* 6*d.*

⁂ *A List of Illustrated Books suitable for Presentation will be forwarded on application.*

London: JAMES HOGG & SON, York Street, Covent Garden, W.C.

www.ingramcontent.com/pod-product-compliance
Lightning Source LLC
LaVergne TN
LVHW010156110826
845151LV00002B/537

* 9 7 8 1 4 2 5 5 3 6 4 3 5 *